# The
# Philosopher's
## Demise

## Books by Richard Watson

THE DOWNFALL OF CARTESIANISM

MAN AND NATURE with Patty Jo Watson

THE LONGEST CAVE with Roger W. Brucker

UNDER PLOWMAN'S FLOOR, a novel

THE RUNNER, a novel

THE PHILOSOPHER'S DIET

THE BREAKDOWN OF CARTESIAN METAPHYSICS

THE PHILOSOPHER'S JOKE

WRITING PHILOSOPHY

NIAGARA, a novel

# LEARNING FRENCH

# The Philosopher's Demise

# Richard Watson

**University of Missouri Press**

Columbia and London

Copyright © 1995 by

The Curators of the University of Missouri

University of Missouri Press, Columbia, Missouri 65201

Printed and bound in the United States of America

All rights reserved

5  4  3  2  1       99  98  97  96  95

**Library of Congress Cataloging-in-Publication Data**

Watson, Richard A., 1931–

    The Philosopher's Demise (Learning French) / Richard Watson.

      p.     cm.

    ISBN 0-8262-1003-1

    1. Watson, Richard A., 1931– —Journeys—France—Paris.  2. Paris (France)—Social life and customs—20th century.  3. French language—Study and teaching—English speakers.  4. French language—Study and teaching—France—Paris.  5. Novelists, American—20th century—Biography.  6. College teachers—United States—Biography.  7. Americans—Travel—France—Paris.  8. Alliance française.  I. Title.

PS3573.A8576Z47   1995

818.5403—dc20                                                     94-42803

  [B]                                                                            CIP

♾ This paper meets the requirements of the

American National Standard for Permanence of Paper

for Printed Library Materials, Z39.48, 1984.

*Designer: Stephanie Foley*

*Typesetter: Bookcomp*

*Printer and binder: Thomson-Shore, Inc.*

*Typefaces: Madrone and Minion*

That's *it?*

**D**emise . . . to transfer . . . to convey . . .
to transmit by succession or inheritance . . .
to pass on.

# The Philosopher's Demise

In September 1950, I registered for a course titled "Reading French." I was nineteen years old, a sophomore at the State University of Iowa, and one year of foreign language was required for graduation. *State* has long since been dropped, so it is no longer SUI, pronounced "ess you eye." But I am pleased to say that at the University of Iowa a year of language is still required for graduation. To be sure, the choice now includes artificial computer languages. I can hardly object because the "Reading French" I learned in 1950–1951 was a language no less artificial than, say, PASCAL, although no one at SUI told me this or perhaps was even aware of it at the time.

I loved learning to read this new language. It was all in the mind. The instructor devoted, at most, fifteen minutes of the first class period to French pronunciation, but we were never required to speak or write the language, only to read it. I read it very well, earning an A for the yearlong, ten-hour course. Moreover, some years later when I took the Ph.D. reading exam in French, I scored 100 percent. This performance was naturally viewed with suspicion by the professor in charge, and although I do not at all remember the instructors who taught the course, I remember quite well the severe purse of the professor's lips when I went— at her urgent request—to see her after the Ph.D. reading exam had been corrected. She did not accuse me of cheating, which is somewhat surprising because in those ancient days the possibility of being sued by a student for defamation of character was unheard of. She wondered if the exam had gotten out beforehand. Not to my knowledge. She wondered if, in the interests of cross-checking, I would be willing to take another exam, right then, in her office. Sure, why not? She produced it, and while she watched, I tried to conceal my amusement in finding that almost all the examples in this new exam were taken from *Les Trois Mousquetaires,* a book I knew well. In any event, the exam was a piece of cake. I handed it to her without checking it over in what I knew was a scandalously short period of time, and was dismissed. Some days later I received notice that "Ph.D. Reading French: Pass" had been posted to my transcript. I was not told my score on the cross-check exam.

Despite the language requirement and the passing of exams, not many graduate students in America could then (or can now) actually read a foreign language. My ability to read French well thus played some part in my decision to write my Ph.D. dissertation in the history of philosophy on Simon Foucher and the later Cartesians. Another reason was that the research for this subject could be done only at the Bibliothèque Nationale in Paris.

The reading room of the Bibliothèque Nationale is an enormous oval. It is divided by an aisle off which rows of reading desks extend at right angles. When you enter you are given a desk number either to the left on a white card or to the right on a green card. Then your dealings for books are with the women at the main desk, right or left.

I dreaded getting a green card because the woman in charge of green tortured me. This began the first day when I asked her a question. She looked at me as though I were an idiot, shook her head, and turned away. When I persisted, she corrected my pronunciation loudly, and made me repeat after her. In the library! In the Bibliothèque Nationale! She stated to the reading room public at large her belief that because I could not speak French, obviously I could not read it. I was wasting her time by requesting that she get books for me. Although I could barely speak French, I understood what she was saying, and eventually I got my books. Thereafter when my card was green and I had to go to the desk, she would stop whatever she was doing to ask me what I wanted, behavior both very un-French (usually they ignore you) and very French, for she delighted in going through the whole routine over and over again. It was humiliating, but I finished my research, wrote the dissertation (in English), published a book based on it, and over the years earned a modest reputation as a Cartesian scholar. I went to France to do library research now and then, and although my ability to speak French improved slightly and I became very good at understanding French spoken to me, I never felt any great need to make a serious effort to learn to speak French, no more than had my former professors and language teachers at SUI felt any need to make me learn to speak (as well as read) the language in the first place.

My career as a Cartesian scholar proceeded calmly for twenty-five years. I did research on original materials in French, reviewed French books, criticized severely one translation into English from the French, and even translated several items from the French myself. During all those years I was never seriously handicapped by my near inability to speak French. Then, in December 1986, I was invited to give a paper the following June at the Centre National de la Recherche Scientifique in Paris at a conference celebrating the three hundred and fiftieth anniversary of the publication of Descartes's *Discours de la Méthode*. The director of the conference was sure that all participants would want to present their papers in French. If any foreign invitees felt shaky about it, he would be glad to go over their manuscripts to shape them up. I could get a colleague in the Romance Languages Department to do that. My problem would be in reading the paper out loud, and answering questions, in French.

I was trapped. I was going to have to learn to speak French.

I went to Michel Rybalka, a professor of French at Washington University, where I taught. He said that attending a class in French for a semester was not enough. Nor would the language course—which his wife, Maya, taught—at the Alliance Française in St. Louis be enough.

"What you must do," he said, "is take tutoring from Maya. She is Basque," he went on, "but her French is perfect."

Maya and I decided on hourlong sessions, Monday, Wednesday, Friday. She would charge only half her usual hourly rate because I was a friend and colleague. I restrained myself from saying that she should not treat me as a special case. I felt guilty about it, but it was her decision, and obviously I was a special case.

The first hour was excruciating. I could not make the sounds. I could hear crucial differences only with difficulty. Maya was cheerful and patient.

"I've had worse," she said encouragingly.

She began with the standard Alliance Française method, having me repeat simple phrases in simple conversations. I could not imagine how someone who knew no French at all could learn to say sentences whose meaning they did not know, or whose meaning was only vaguely apparent in the context of the pictures in the text. I could barely tolerate it, and I knew what we were saying.

"That's just your problem," Maya said. "Concentrate solely on the sounds and forget the meaning."

I tried, but I had always hated nonsense memory games. I found it nearly impossible to pick up phrases and patterns by sound alone. If I didn't understand it, I couldn't remember it.

At the end of the second hour I said, "I can't believe very many people go through with this. Most people won't impose this much stress on themselves. They'll quit."

"Some students do quit in the first week," Maya said. "But others like it."

By the end of the second week, I could make all the sounds correctly. But my knowing too much French was a serious problem.

"I never knew anyone who knew French so well and couldn't speak a word," Maya said.

"Quit visualizing the words!" she scolded when I stumbled and stopped to think.

"I'm *not* visualizing," I cried. "Would that I were! Then I could read right off what I want to say."

I had an enormous reading vocabulary, but I could not connect it to my minuscule speaking vocabulary. When I tried to say something, the words eluded me. They did not come up mispronounced, they did not come up at all, I suppose because I read French rapidly, passing over the printed words without imagining any sounds at all, going directly from print to meaning. Some years before, I had noticed—not without pride—that I could be reading a book consciously unaware as to whether it was in French or English. But that entire sight-recognition vocabulary was useless to me in my attempt to speak French. Now I had to slow down and concentrate on the sounds. I started reading French out loud.

These beginnings were during the last two weeks in December. Already I was in a panic. There wasn't going to be enough time. When the new year started, I added an hour on Saturday. I bought a Walkman recorder and listened to tapes while going to and from the classes I had to teach. I listened at home. I was not going to get anything else done during the spring semester, I could see that. Writing the paper for the conference would be nothing compared to preparing to deliver it.

"Because I never had the time, there was always too much else to do," I snapped at my mother when I visited her at Christmas. She had asked the reasonable question of why I had never bothered to learn to speak French before.

The tenseness of trying increased. I was very slow.

"At least you can make all the sounds," Maya said brightly. "Some people never get them all."

"I'll have to increase the fees," she said after the holidays. That seemed reasonable to me.

"Actually, we didn't think you'd go through with it," she went on.

I had been depressed with humiliation for two weeks. Now I was stunned. Maya and Michel had seen my ambition as an amusement. I had been humored. That was why she had cut her rate in half. She didn't want me to waste too much money. But now it was going to take time, her time. She advanced her fee to three-quarters her normal rate.

"Is that . . . right?" I asked. I had started to say "enough."

"Yes," she said, "that's enough. Your case is an interesting challenge."

And then we went to work in earnest. She was the teacher, I was the student.

All my life I have inhabited the world of teachers and students. My father was a secondary school teacher, coach, and superintendent in small towns in Iowa for forty-five years. Thirteen of my uncles and aunts were teachers. My wife, my brother and his wife, and many of my cousins are teachers. I started school when I was five years old and was thirty when I received my Ph.D. Even one of the two years I was in the Air Force I went to school. I met Pat (who later became my wife) in a classroom when she was thirteen and I was fourteen. She received her Ph.D. when she was twenty-eight. We have been college teachers now for over twenty-five years, and have another ten or fifteen to go before retirement. My life has been one of nearly total immersion in academe, and all that time I have been either a student or a teacher.

But I had not been a student for twenty-five years. Once I decided to do it, however, the ambition to learn to speak French became an obsession. Had Maya only known my true nature, she would never have given me a trial run at half price. And how could Michel, who did know me, have described me to her as a quitter? Learning to speak French was for me a deadly serious matter, like dieting and exploring caves.

It was also like diving naked and alone into ice water. I was frozen with panic. I found to my horror that I was not an able student, as I always had been before. Was I really too old? They say you should learn languages young, that it is easier then. The ear and tongue grow less flexible as they age. My fifty-five-year-old ear and tongue were stiff as boards. But I knew what was required, and if the quickness of youth was gone, the staying power of age was not. I would beat myself into shape.

Maya and I met in her home. Books, papers, and tape recorders were spread on the lace tablecloth of the dining room table. We labored three then four then five times a week, and then every day for the last three weeks before I flew to Paris to give my paper. Her three teenage children came home from school and she held her cheek up absently to be bussed. Michel came in to linger over mail left for him on the corner of the table. The large brown rabbit Ttunttululun (which in Basque means "sweet silly thing") scratched frantically on the closed kitchen door, wanting to go in or come out, determined to take that route although there was—as he perfectly well knew—an open passage between the dining room and the kitchen through a back hall. Maya ignored him if he was in the kitchen, sighed and got up absently to let him through if he was in the dining room. She picked him up and hugged him, kissing the top of his head, warning everyone else that he bites.

"Michel is terrified of him," she said, delighted.

The telephone rang—she ignored it—her children yelled downstairs at her in anguish—"Not when I'm teaching! You know not when I'm teaching!"—but it was her mother on the phone long-distance from France—she took the call.

The weather got hotter and hotter. It was going to be one of those years in St. Louis where you look back and say, "Oh yes, we had spring. It was on the twelfth of April."

Before air-conditioning, the British consul, when there was one in St. Louis, got tropical hardship pay for the Missouri summer.

I continued to push myself with the comforting conviction that very few adults would submit themselves to such torture. Nor children, for that matter; their parents force them.

I wrote my paper, but it had to be translated into French. I could easily have asked Michel to translate it. True, no more than Maya was he fully French. Maya pointed out that his parents were Ukrainian. Never mind, his field was contemporary French literature, and he was an expert on Jean-Paul Sartre. That was French enough for me. Instead, I translated the paper myself. Maya corrected it. Then Michel took it upstairs and shouted down arguments about grammar. As for presenting the paper, Maya was in Paris on the date of the conference. She would have been glad to read the paper for me, and I have no doubt that she could have fielded all the questions. I had not needed to speak French for all those years. I did not need to speak French now. Why was I doing it?

I was awarded my Eagle Scout badge when I was fifteen, which was congruent with the prescribed time limitations that began with Tenderfoot at age twelve. One of the merit badges required to reach the exalted Eagle rank was Hiking. I forget how many ten-mile hikes you had to take, but the final requirement was a twenty-mile hike. It is incredibly boring to take hikes in rural Iowa for the same reason that it is easy to measure them, because the land is ruled out in exact one-mile squares. There was no temptation to cut corners, as anyone who has ever tried to walk kitty-corner across a cornfield knows. Lyle Tabat, Dick Gamm, and I trudged out our complement of ten-mile hikes, which were, as I recall, extremely wearing as well as dull. This puzzles me now because we were on the high school basketball and baseball teams and were, one would have thought, in good shape. Gamm and I (we always called each other by our last names) were of normal size for fifteen-year-old boys, but Tabat was a year or two older and was already well on his way to six foot four. He kept yelling at us to hurry up. Our ten-mile hikes were hot, dirty, and interminable. Today, like many professional people with energy to burn, I can, more than forty years later, *run* ten miles with no effort at all. But those hikes at fifteen were hard.

For our twenty-mile hike, we decided to walk from our hometown to the next larger town. Depending on where you start and end, the distance from Sheffield to Mason City is no less than sixteen and no more than eighteen miles. We hiked probably about seventeen. It was not a twenty-mile hike. We knew it, and the scoutmaster who gave us our Hiking merit badges knew it. I have never felt right about it. That is why after being a Cartesian scholar for more than twenty-five years, I now had to learn to speak French.

"Bonjour," I greeted Maya each day. But in all those six months I never once said "Bonjour" to her satisfaction. I could make the proper *j* sound in other words, even in "journal," but I could not say "Bonjour." Her three kids trailed in and each one said, "Bonjour." Maya corrected my reply. As the months went by, Maya's strength as a teacher began to loom over me like a cage of steel. She never seemed impatient. She never skipped over anything. She never let anything go.

"Bonjour."

"No, it is 'Bonjour.' The *j* is farther back on your tongue. Watch my tongue. 'Bonjour.' Now you try it."

I despaired. How could someone who couldn't even greet a Frenchman properly expect to speak French? I had never set out to learn something before that I had not eventually mastered. So why couldn't I learn this?

"Bonjour! Bonjour! Bonjour!"

"You *can* make the sounds correctly," Maya said. "Pay attention, *exaggerate,* and then you get them right."

She threw up her hands. "I don't *believe* it! You talk without moving your mouth. You have to *work* to speak French. Watch my mouth. *Reach* for the sounds."

Maya was a handsome, vivacious, enormously energetic woman, with flashing eyes and an imposing Gallic (Basque?) nose. It flustered me to watch her mouth. Beyond that, it was clear that it embarrassed me to speak French. I knew exactly why that was. I didn't want to sound like Charles Boyer in the movies of my childhood. We hooted and groaned when he breathed down the neck of some woman on the screen. And there was the suggestion that he might do things to them offscreen that no real man would ever be caught dead doing.

A great suspicion came over me: Real Men Don't Speak French. But just as you must survive humiliation and submit to agonizing tension, so also must you overcome embarrassment. Make an ass of yourself. If you want to learn.

The textbook consisted of twenty-eight lessons, mostly phrases and conversations. We made our way through the book, barely completing it before I left for France. Maya read a few words, or, often, because she had taught it so many times, she just said them, knowing them by heart. I repeated. Maya corrected me. I repeated again. On to the next phrase.

I focused my attention heavily on the work at hand, as did she. Often the hour would stretch to an hour and a half without our remarking it. She surely noticed, as did I—after all, teachers and students know the passing of an hour— but neither of us said anything. We knew I needed the extra time. Then Maya would say, "Oh! I must fix dinner," and we would stop.

You know those advertisements promising that you can speak a foreign language like a native or a diplomat in just a few easy lessons? What a laugh.

The six months of tutoring with Maya neared their end. The Rybalkas gave a reception for their students at the close of the school year. The table was laden with wonderful things to eat. Maya had made the Basque cake I loved. The cheerfulness and conviviality were overwhelming. Everyone spoke French. Of course it was at the farthest remove from France, and went to confirm Michel's claim that Maya was really Basque and Maya's claim that Michel was really Ukrainian, because no truly French professor from the beginning of time has ever laid out such a spread for students.

I arrived in Paris four days before I was to give my paper. Maya had read it on tape for me, and I listened to it and repeated it several times a day. The night before delivery day, I timed myself. It took fifty-five minutes. I had thirty-five. Far into the early hours of morning I sweated over cutting it down, a grammar book at my elbow. It was going to be all right. I knew what I was doing.

Finally I stood up to read my paper. I wore my black suit and vest, tailored of the best (thickest) English wool in Kermanshah, Iran, in 1959. It was like new because I almost never wore a suit, and it was of a cut that always elicited comment. Thank God early June in Paris was cool. Once onstage, I was calm, but the loudspeaker system startled me because it threw my voice back as though it belonged to someone else. I began listening and correcting my pronunciation until at the end the air was twanging with nasals and vibrating with rrrs. I read my paper in twenty-five minutes, but the moderator was grateful because he had not been able to stop another reader who had gone on for an hour. I understood the questions that were asked after my paper, but when I started to answer them my mind looked with horror into the bottomless pit of echoing silence where every word of French I had ever known had sunk into oblivion like a lost chord. I had to answer in English.

My French was far from the worst among the foreigners. On any fair assessment, it was among the best. I noticed that the other American, who spoke far more fluently than I, did not make the elisions between words that are essential for speaking colloquial French. Elisions, incidently, make it difficult to go from written to spoken French because the sound units so often consist of the last part of the preceding word and only the first part of the operating word. Thus the meaning units of sound overlap and are different from those of the written word.

The distinguished English historian of science didn't do accents. Instead, he read French words as though they were English, with particular stress on all the endings that are silent in French.

"That'll bloody well set them straight," someone whispered in English behind me.

The Italian read his paper with Italian accents, the Japanese with Japanese gutturals and deletions, and the Spaniard was halfway through his paper before anyone realized that he was reading it in French, not in Spanish. All in all, I was quite pleased with myself, except for having to answer my questions in English. On a scale of 1 to 10, I thought I surely rated no lower than an 8, whereas the Englishman got a 6 for having to have the questions translated for him into English, although he did then, sort of, answer them in French. But I had no illusions. I could not really speak French.

This was clear to me the first day of the conference. I went early to let the director know I was there. He introduced me to Professor Marion, with whom he was talking. That was great, I was quite interested in Marion's work. After hearing me say "Bonjour," he spoke to me in English.

"Your long review was perceptive," Professor Marion said.

Good, he knew the piece I'd published about two of his books.

"I hope we'll get a chance to talk," I said.

"Yes," he said, "but I'm very busy today. We'll get together tomorrow."

I laughed. Scholars at conferences are like chickens in a barnyard. Every one of them chases from place to place, always thinking the pecking will be better somewhere else.

Squawk! What have those two birds with their heads down got hold of over there?

Professor Marion was gone.

The next day he said, "I'm very busy right now, let's get together in a couple of hours."

There were more big roosters here than at most conferences. I enjoyed watching them strut and preen. I was careful to keep to the edges so I wouldn't have to do any clucking myself.

The third and final day, Professor Marion said, "I've got to see someone right now. Can you wait another few minutes?"

Again he was gone.

The last I saw of Professor Marion, he was leaving the conference. He happened to look right at me in a last appraising survey just before he went out the door. I flapped my wings, but he had had enough chicken feed.

Perhaps it was just as well. All I had learned in six months of tutoring was how to read French out loud. If I had not already known this, three days at the conference would have convinced me. At the end I could not even speak the few words and sentences that had always been my mainstays in France. Something deep in me dictated that it was better to say nothing, to be thought bereft of any spoken French, than to expose the limited extent of what I knew. Moreover, to my horror, I discovered that if I did try to use the bits of spoken French that had served me in the past, all the old mispronunciations remained. My new knowledge of how to make the sounds had not transferred. I remained silent and watched the show.

Most interesting were one or two big—I mean really important—men of the type who always bring along their wives. These are not professional women—that is, they are not themselves scholars. They attend so many meetings and hear so many papers that often they can engage in shoptalk, but it is not their shop. They would rather talk about the museums and monuments of the conference city, or drop names, and gossip. These wives are charming. The young men flock around them. Always in range, but seldom at her side, hovers the big man. But I don't mean to suggest at all that his wife—even when she is the third, or a third his age, and extremely ornamental—is just an ornament. She is to him like a cigarette to a smoker, who would be nervous if the nicotine did not give him courage. She is the apparently frivolous but absolutely essential sticky ingredient in the big man's mixture without which he would fall apart. This is not a simple relationship, nor an easy job for such wives. I watched and wished one of them would talk to me.

I cared too much. My wife, Pat, is an archaeologist and has worked in Iraq, Iran, and Turkey. She is good at languages and has studied Arabic, Farsi, Kurdish, and Turkish as well as French, Spanish, and German. But often in the Near East, she would be tongue-tied while I blithely carried on conversations with the few hundred words and rudimentary grammar that I had gleaned from that wonderful and I am afraid now defunct series of blue-backed books titled *Teach Yourself Persian,* or whatever language you wanted to speak. One could not say that I really spoke Kurdish, for example, but I communicated enthusiastically and well enough. With time to think, Pat could speak these languages correctly, but I just talked, any old way.

The other American who delivered a paper at the conference, Dan Garber, was twenty years my junior. He wandered around the conference halls and—with no more formal training in French than I had—spoke French with more and more facility from one day to the next.

"Oh, if I could only stay here for six weeks," he said, "I know I would be speaking French fluently."

I grunted. I was afraid it was probably true, although I permitted myself a thought about the flatness of his nasals and his ubiquitous utilization of the present tense.

Dan was doing my old thing. I knew and cared too much to be able to do that now.

At the final session, the conference director thanked all the foreigners for having made the effort to read their papers in the very difficult language of Descartes. Discounting French sarcasm, I thought the director's even suggesting that some foreigners might not naturally speak French must represent one of the lowest points to which French culture and confidence has descended at least since Descartes's *Discours* was published in 1637.

**A**t the reception closing the conference Willis Doney, a senior American Cartesian scholar who had an apartment in Paris and spoke French well, invited me to go the next day with him and Madame Geneviève Rodis-Lewis to another Descartes conference. It was to be held in the village of Descartes, formerly La-Haye-Descartes, and before that, when Descartes was born there in 1596, La Haye. Professor Rodis-Lewis was to be, as she had been at this conference, a major speaker. She was—except for Henri Gouhier, who seemed destined to fulfill Descartes's dream of living and publishing into his hundredth year—the most distinguished living French Cartesian scholar. She was a petite woman approaching seventy with tinted auburn hair in a fashionable cap-cut. She always had been an absolute knockout; her tilted head and laughing eyes, painted pixie smile, and expensive green silk suit made it clear that she had no intention whatsoever of letting age dim the glow. She had published many books on Descartes, all of them essential.

Professor Rodis-Lewis knew all there was to know about Descartes. She talked your arms and legs off at a breathtaking pace, laughing and smiling and pushing back her hair. She was the ocean, and at both conferences there were these little men standing on the beach, casting in their pebbles of interpretation and critique, years in the making, while she, chattering like little choppy waves, swallowed them all without pause, without notice, so they sank like balls of lead, and made no impression at all. Underneath, there was the deep, the mighty swell. She had thought it, knew it, said it, already, all. And this despite recovering from a very recent and very serious operation on her liver that she described so graphically that I'm still uncertain that she did not, like President Johnson, hoist up her shirtwaist and show us the scar.

Professor Doney of Dartmouth College was equal to his role as her traveling companion. A big man of Scandinavian descent, he was a lifelong bachelor somewhere in his sixties, six foot three inches tall with thin blond hair, a large full face, large washed blue eyes, large ears, large hands and feet and thighs. He wore an expensive gray English wool suit, a black belted French raincoat, and a checkered MG cap. He used a cane to compensate for a trick knee and the treacheries of fine French wine. As a Cartesian scholar, he was as well known in America as was Professor Rodis-Lewis in France, and he had recently edited a fifteen-volume set of reprints of the most important commentaries that included some of her work. He came as close to being accepted in that golden circle of French Cartesian scholars as anyone who was not one of them could ever hope to be, and I envied him.

Traveling with us in the first-class compartment of the train from Paris to Châtellerault, where we would be met and taken on by private automobile to the village now called Descartes, was a Japanese Cartesian scholar, Professor Michjio Kobayshi, who noticed nothing unusual about my spoken French. We talked to one another easily in French. Professor Rodis-Lewis also chatted with me at length, responding to my French without hesitation, but I was not sure that she actually tried to understand. With her, one had not so much a talk, as a listen.

Our train arrived at the provincial station of Châtellerault. Madame Rodis-Lewis showed with great sweeps of her elegantly taloned hands where she had been cut open so could not carry her own bags. Professor Doney fumbled with his pipe and cane. I shooed them out, and Professor Kobayshi and I followed, carrying all the luggage. We were met by the retired French army general who was in charge of logistics for the conference and who instantly took everyone's measure. The general opened the trunk of his car so that Kobayshi and I could deposit the luggage, and then he swept Madame Rodis-Lewis and Professor Doney off. Kobayshi and I packed ourselves into the much smaller car of Professor Jean-Henri Roy, the local Cartesian scholar, who took off in pursuit of the general.

Professor Roy taught at the college in Châtellerault, where Descartes's father and grandfather had lived. When he was a young man, Professor Roy had worked with Sartre, contributing criticism to the periodical *Les Temps Modernes.* He was now an expert on the Descartes family, and so combined the best aspects of a local village explainer with the accuracy of a scholar. I already knew Professor Roy through correspondence about a book I was writing titled *The Death of Descartes.* We greeted each other with great pleasure and instant affection.

"You will stay here to work this summer," he said.

I could not, but I promised to return later so he could show me the extensive former properties of the Descartes family, and so we could go through the remaining documents together. Professor Roy talked about Descartes as he drove the eighteen miles to the village and, like Professor Kobayshi, had no trouble with my French.

The general pulled up in front of the best hotel in town, with Professor Roy close behind him. Professor Doney had not been expected, but the general quickly arranged a room for him. Then, after supervising our unloading of the baggage, he gestured vaguely at Kobayshi and me and said there were cheaper accommodations down the street. I had been in the village before and knew the small hotel over a bar he meant, so I led the way.

I was wearing tan chino trousers, a blue dress shirt, a blue sleeveless sweater, my red-green-and-blue Washington University tie, and a brown hopsack sport coat I had purchased in Albuquerque in 1958. It has not worn badly, but I don't actually wear a sport coat much, and I've not seen one since that I liked as well. Professor Kobayshi was wearing a dark suit. Later, Professor Doney told me that to his great embarrassment, the general had insisted on paying for his hotel room. I understood.

All of us, including Madame Rodis-Lewis, were wearing black shoes. I had purchased a pair only a few years before after a meeting of deans, members of the university board of trustees, and a few faculty members, at which I noticed that I was the only man wearing brown shoes. I might go on to say that, on a later occasion in such company, newly and, I thought, appropriately shod, I noticed that the soles of my new black shoes were thicker than those of any other man's present. This was because my soles were rubber. Could the dividing line actually be so thin, between those who can keep their balance on slick parquet floors while wearing leather soles, and those who cannot?

The Descartes conference in Descartes was held in the community hall. It was an affair of a sort hard to visualize taking place in America. But imagine Burlington, Vermont, where John Dewey was born, now renamed Dewey. And in Dewey, all the local town fathers are steeped in his works, and can quote him appropriately on whatever occasion. And, say, on the one hundredth anniversary of the publication of *The Quest for Certainty,* they sponsor a conference to which they invite important Dewey scholars to present papers. It is held in the community center and is attended enthusiastically by a large number of local residents, some of whom ask knowledgeable questions during discussion periods.

At the close of the Descartes conference in Descartes, there was a reception with large bottles of the best local wine. We had already been served much fine wine and fine cuisine at two official luncheons and two dinners, all four meals running to seven courses. Now the mayor, the president of Les Amis de Descartes, and the director of the local Descartes museum all made lengthy, congratulatory speeches, smiling and gesticulating wildly, concluding with the presentation to Professors Doney, Kobayshi, and me of bronze medallions embossed with the bust of Descartes and a view of his natal village, for making their conference international. Professor Roy again reminded me of my promise—I shall return. The three town fathers assured me that they would do everything possible to make my research on Descartes in Descartes profitable. The general shook my hand.

I was charmed. What more, in God's name, did I want?

What I wanted, was that when I asked a distinguished Cartesian scholar a question, as I did in a discussion period at the conference in Descartes, but had not dared to do in Paris, what I wanted was that he understand and answer my question, that he not look as though the village idiot had spoken to him with all the earnestness of his imbecility and as clearly as a cleft palate permitted. I wanted finally that Professor Roy would not have to repeat my question to the distinguished professor for me in virtually the same words I had used, and what I wanted was that the distinguished Cartesian scholar did not then lift his eyebrows, roll his eyes to the ceiling, shake his head, and say, "I wouldn't know how to answer that," and then turn quickly to field with great courtesy a puerile question from a local resident, who, for all I know, may have been the village moron, if not the village idiot.

I would return to Châtellerault, to the kindness and friendship of Professor Roy, and we would pursue together our research on the family Descartes. I would respect the sincere interest and pride of the Descartes village fathers. But, let's face it. This was the minor leagues. Softball. Now I was going back to Paris where they played hardball.

It was early June and I was fancy-free in Paris. Not bad for a boy from the sticks. Pat was not coming to France until August. I planned to do some research and writing at the Bibliothèque Nationale. And, you know, hang out.

But Maya had said, "When you get to Paris, you really should take a course at the Alliance Française." And where would someone my age hang out, anyway? With the cheerless and heavy tread of a man who finishes what he starts, I made my way to the Alliance Française on rue Raspail.  BLVD

The placement exam was multiple choice as in days of old. I could read it well enough, but I often had to guess which of several slightly differing grammatical constructions was correct. I did as well as I could.

"No," the woman said expressionlessly after she had corrected it.

"No, what?"

"No, you don't know enough French to enter a class."

"But what's the problem?" I asked. "I thought you took students at all levels."

"No."

"Look," I said, "we have been talking in French. I understand you and, as bad as my French is, you understand me. Isn't that enough?"

The French are, if anything, logical. She looked at me thoughtfully and then said she would go ask. When she came back she said nothing, but registered me for Part II of a four-part intensive introductory course, four hours a day, five days a week, for four months. I would enter the second month. I did not know at the time that this was what she had done, but in fact this was—after six months with Maya—about the right level for me.

"Good luck," she said to me, in English, as I left.

I dived in that afternoon, one week late in a section of Part II.

At all times there are about a hundred and thirty teachers and two or three thousand students at the Alliance Française in Paris. Most of the students are enrolled in the introductory course. You must pass an exam at the end of each month to go on to the next, and at the end of the fourth month you must pass a comprehensive exam. If you pass the exam at the end of four months, you are given, or rather sold, a diploma suitable for framing certifying that you have attained proficiency in French. Many foreigners work toward this diploma for use in getting jobs requiring French in their home countries, and many French employers require it of their foreign employees. In my three months of classes, my fellow students were American, Canadian, English, Mexican, Colombian, Brazilian, Swedish, Irish, Polish, German, Austrian, Swiss,

Belgian, Dutch, Romanian, Turkish, Greek, Italian, Spanish, Iranian, Syrian, North African, Filipino, Korean, Vietnamese, and Japanese. There were twenty-five to thirty students in each class. Their average age was about twenty. Half were college students, and the others were mostly teachers like me or foreigners working in Paris. I was thirty or more years older than most of my fellow students.

When I entered at the beginning of the second week of the second month, five minutes late, having just rushed over from paying my fee, the teacher stopped talking when I walked in. She was a woman of thirty or so with bushy brown hair and bright black eyes. She wore a thin white blouse and a flouncing pleated brown skirt that swelled over her haunch as she stood with one hand on her hip, waiting for me to sit down. She did not have the emaciated Parisian look, that prized cold frowning sexuality that is so common, but smiled at me easily and knowingly, almost an appraising flirtation. She was very pretty, and I liked her at once, something she could obviously see.

"My name is Claire," she said. "Who are you?"

My name was not enough. I was to tell her what I did, why I wanted to learn French, and a little bit about myself. She corrected my French as I stumbled along. Unfortunately, she said, there wasn't time for me to learn about the others who had told who they were the first day of class, I could ask them individually, I had noticed that I was almost a week late? I had.

"She will help you," Claire said, pointing pleasantly to the beautiful Filipino woman sitting next to me. An elegant be-ringed hand was put on my arm briefly as the Filipino woman (about forty, I judged) leaned over to assure me it was true. The very young Colombian girl sitting on my other side whispered, "Are you really a professor of philosophy? I adore philosophy." Seventeen.

They had brown eyes.

I turned back to Claire, who was waiting for me to return my attention to her. She nodded and went back to the explanation I had interrupted. I liked this class.

Claire liked it, too. She was a literature student at the Sorbonne who had us sit with our eyes closed while she read poetry out loud. She was also fond of arranging us in groups of three or four to act out situations. Once when we were to make up our own play, she raved about my three-act, six-minute rendition of Jean Valjean in *Les Misérables.*

Claire talked constantly and got angry when anyone did not pay attention. This was not uncommon because the class sessions were four hours long with a break of only fifteen to twenty minutes, and it was all in French. The sessions were from 12:30 to 4:30, although Claire sometimes kept us until 5:00. No one complained. Most of the students enjoyed what she did. Situations.

"All right, Christine, John is trying to pick you up and you give him reasons why you aren't interested and he gives you reasons why you should be."

"Richard," she said to me with her eyes twinkling, "this young couple has marital problems." She smirked. "You are a wise old married man and they come to you and tell you their problems and you give them advice."

Each of us had to give a fifteen-minute presentation. The best was by a very wide Brazilian woman about fifty years old, my only contemporary in the class. She told about the Mardis Gras in Rio de Janeiro and passed around posters and a picture book.

"Did you ever parade like this?" Claire asked, holding up a large poster of a nearly naked woman riding post on top of a tall float in the form of a horse.

"Oh, yes, yes," the woman laughed. "But there wasn't so much of me then," she said, shaking her shoulders.

Claire was very partial to a Brazilian boy about eighteen. He was everyone's favorite, as had been determined once when Claire ran a popularity contest. She had ruled herself out of that contest, but when she had us write character sketches, almost everyone wrote about her. The Brazilian boy talked, interrupted, and was as unselfconsciously full of himself as a handsome young stag. One day he was stretching and smiling and yawning, looking around to attract attention, when suddenly Claire blew up.

"Do you think I am not tired?" she asked. "All of us are tired." She was furious. "You think it is easy to teach a class like this? New students enter all during the month. They quit and don't even say good-bye, just as though I were not a person, but a piece of the furniture. Everybody is on a different level. It is impossible. Then I have to look at your stupid yawning face. Sit up. Pay attention."

He stood up, livid, and protested. They argued. He took a step toward her, then whirled and strode out of the class-room, slamming the door behind him. Claire was close to tears. She sat down behind her desk and held her head in her hands. She so seldom sat down, always parading in the center as we sat in a circle around the room. In a moment she got up and went on grimly. In three minutes her cheerfulness had returned. At the end of the class she asked who knew the Brazilian boy. A German girl did.

"When you go out with him tonight, you tell him to come back. All is forgiven," she said gaily.

There was another week of classes, but he didn't return until the last day. He and Claire greeted each other joyfully.

Claire paid attention to everyone in the class. One day she zeroed in on an ethereal looking Japanese boy about eighteen years old.

She bent over him and asked, "Why don't you ever say anything?"

She turned to the rest of the class. "It is because he is Japanese, you see. He is afraid to make a mistake because that would mean he had lost face. And to a woman," she laughed with delight.

"Now I know you understand because your written work is good." She asked him a grammar question, but he wouldn't speak.

"See," she said gleefully. "I've made him lose face."

Then her mood changed swiftly. "Oh," she said, glancing down at him dismissively, "I know you know the answer perfectly well. You really do have to talk." She turned away.

The Japanese boy did not return after the break nor the next day.

"Where is he?" Claire asked an older Japanese man in the class. "Tell him I was just teasing."

The man replied with solemn Japanese humor that the boy knew that she had been teasing him.

"That is why he won't come back," he went on pensively.

"He has paid a lot of money for this class," Claire snapped. "You tell him to come back or change to another teacher."

When we paid our tuition we had all signed agreements to the effect that under no circumstance either conceivable or inconceivable to the minds of gods or men would there be any refund of our money.

The next day he was back, and a few days later he answered a question. Claire asked us to tell in turn whom we liked and disliked the most. The young Japanese boy said he liked Hitler because he was so strong and he hated women because they were so weak.

The sexual ambience in the classroom was heavy. You know what they say about the best way to learn a foreign language. Claire simply assumed—I saw no evidence to contradict her—that a classroom full of males and females mostly in their late teens and early twenties would be interested in sex and would enjoy all the sexual innuendo, as she did. Certainly after no more than two days of going up to the fourth-floor classroom on those crowded stairways and through those packed halls, I had already decided that the Alliance Française must be one of the greatest places for exotic pickups in the Western world. I was told that French boys sometimes signed up for classes for that very reason.

The French clearly have not grasped the concept of sexual harassment. Claire, for example. I liked her more and more as the days went by, and nothing of that sort escaped her scrutiny for an instant. So she teased me. And isn't that how some male professors in America get in trouble? Not that they are serious, you understand, they are just teasing. I liked being teased. But the young Japanese boy hated it, and I doubt that Claire was ever serious about it.

Probably most men would enjoy being flirted with by a pretty teacher. It might increase their interest in the course. It certainly made it more pleasant for me, but then I was fifty-five, not eighteen. Which explains partly—my age, that is—but not entirely, why I never picked up one of those exotic women at the Alliance Française. The Colombian girl was lovely and very friendly, but she was younger than my daughter, and I had already resigned myself years ago to being the grandfather they wanted me to be, all those desirable young women who think any man over thirty is over the hill.

The Filipino woman was another matter. She had children the age of the Colombian girl and she was very attentive. So? Well, here it is. Do you have any idea how much it would cost to take a woman out in Paris who wore rings and clothes like hers, and lived in such a house (she showed me photographs)? The sexual fires do dim with age. Slightly, but enough to admit the cold counsels of fiscal prudence. Perhaps when younger I might have forgotten that half pay on sabbatical leave is barely enough to live on.

So says he.

The man who taught the class just before Claire's wore a scrubby, very fashionable, three-day beard. He was in his early thirties, and he was having a ball. One day I entered the classroom early as he was talking to two young female students, both Americans. He gave me a fraternal male wink of confidence. He enjoyed being hustled. I don't suppose the American girls thought of the Alliance Française as really being school, nor of the Frenchman as a real professor.

During my three months at the Alliance Française, I had five different teachers, one for only one day and another for four, but those two made as strong an impression as the other three. The one-day substitute was tall and thin, draped here and there in that Parisian way with scarves and cloths in an appearance of randomness and scantiness that is both deceptive and totally contrived. They look loose, but my guess is that such costumes are as hard to take off as to put on.

This one-day replacement was a regular staff member at the Alliance Française, but somehow she had never quite gotten over her amazement that a bunch of tongue-tied foreigners could communicate at all. She seemed genuinely embarrassed at our febrile efforts and would tentatively try to help—as none of the other teachers ever did—by dropping in a word from one of our own languages here and there to encourage us, always some utterly common word such as *door* or *policeman* in German or Italian that was of no help at all. All of us were quite amazed, and outraged, that a language teacher, of all people, would succumb to the pathetic fallacy of thinking that people who cannot speak her language are not quite bright.

There were too many students in the Alliance Française sections. Ten minutes after the first class of Part III (my second month) was supposed to begin, a flustered official herded us into an adjoining classroom—we were urged to take our chairs with us—already occupied by thirty students. Their teacher in an absentminded and nearsighted way raised her voice to continue her lecture. She ignored us and the uproar we made. About the time we were settled, the door crashed open again and a tall gangly woman dressed in a black suit hunched her head and shoulders into the room, nodding and smiling—she looked like Jacques Tati in the role of Mr. Hulot on holiday—and said in a hoarse whisper that she had bronchitis, which was a terrible affliction for a professor, but she hoped to see us in a day or two. She was immensely cheerful about this, and nodded to the teacher whose class we had invaded. This woman made no response, but she had stopped talking while being interrupted by our rasping professor.

The classroom was now packed with over fifty students sitting in chairs around all four sides of the room. The teacher walked constantly from the front of her desk to the midpoint of the room and then backward to her desk again, feeling for it behind her with her hand. She would pause against it a moment, then move forward again. She appeared not to see with any assurance past the end of her nose, but as she made her cautious forays into empty space and back, she still seemed to be seeking out specific students settled in the distant reaches of the room. She seldom addressed students to the side and never looked at those behind her. As she lectured she had the nervous habit of repeating "bon" ("good") after every phrase, as many Americans fill in the empty spaces of talk with "ah."

It was soon apparent that she was trying to address only those students who were assigned to her section, and to ask questions only of those among them who already knew the material she was presenting. She manifested profound distress when someone did not know the answer to a question. When that happened she rushed quickly, not to another student, but to give the answer herself. One result was that if our one-day teacher had annoyed everyone by treating us as though we looked perfectly normal but were pitifully feebleminded, this teacher annoyed almost everyone in her ineffectual attempts to ignore half of us and to spare all of us the shame of making a mistake.

She was very businesslike in going through the material, but, I thought, self-conscious to a degree that made students uncomfortable. This impression was dispelled when all at once, during the third hour, this clumsy, dumpy, thirtyish woman acted out for us the meaning of the word *coquette*. The transformation was spectacular, and brought home to me again the truth that all Frenchwomen believe the scuttlebutt that all Frenchwomen are sexy and beautiful. When they remember this—as our teacher apparently just had— they really are. Czech women are so sexy as to make you gasp as though the blade of a knife had been slipped between your ribs. Swedish girls are the most coyly lovely on earth. But

Frenchwomen—their size, shape, and age being irrelevant—
are the most beautiful.

This reminder did rather seem to buck her up. I realized
that she was not nervous or uneasy at all, but just fatigued.
Four hours with only a twenty-minute break is a long time
to be center stage, particularly when you are the only one
who knows the lines, and here on the very first day of a new
class she had twenty-five extra students dumped onto her.

During the four days the two classes were together, she
doggedly reviewed all the grammar we were supposed to
have had during the preceding two months. Having entered
late, I appreciated this, and it was a revelation to some of
my new classmates, whose previous teachers had not stressed
grammar at all, but simply led their classes in conversational
fun and games.

The classroom was noisy. Claire had kept some semblance
of order, but the nearsighted woman ignored disruption.
There was a Romanian boy about twenty whose French was
very good and who talked all the time, to his neighbors, to
the teacher, and to himself. Others tried to ignore or shush
him, but he was irrepressible.

"You know," my neighbor whispered to me, "he does
that because all the students talk all the time in classes in
Romania."

"But what do the professors do?" I asked.

She shrugged her shoulders. "They continue as best they
can."

She was a social anthropologist who worked in Romania
and had suffered it herself.

"You've got to tell him it isn't done here," I told her during the break. "He's making the class impossible."

"It will only make him mad," she said.

But after two days she couldn't take it any longer herself and told him.

He got very angry. "Who needs the stupid class?" he said, and did not come back.

"That's very Romanian, too," she said.

**R**ecovered from her bronchitis, our assigned teacher shepherded most of us back into our classroom, chairs in hand. Two or three of her students had fixated themselves on the nearsighted woman and refused to go. Nothing was said about that as students were changing sections all the time anyway. The teachers' genial smiles when someone transferred out of their classes showed that they were being paid by the month and not by the number of students.

"You should call me 'Professor,' to be sure," our new teacher said when someone asked her after the ritual roundabout during which each student stated name, profession, and life goals.

"Like Richard there," she said, shrugging a shoulder in my direction without looking at me.

I felt a chill. I had, in fact, considered stating my profession as writer, which is true enough except that if I had to make a living at it, I might starve. At the beginning of each new class when in my brave honesty I stated the truth, I knew that I would hear about it one way or another, particularly given that I was always near the bottom of the class. Even

Claire, after I had shushed her and told her I would give my required presentation in my own way, said in a tone of voice from which not quite all skepticism had been removed, "You truly are a professor, aren't you?"

The Professor for Part III of the four-month course in intensive French, four hours a day, five days a week, and more studying and homework than was possible to complete in the time that was left, that tall angular woman of a certain age, looked more English than French. Of the horsey set. She wore that first day, and for three succeeding days, a Mickey Mouse T-shirt and dark slacks. Unlike the other teachers who had students sit facing one another in a circle around the walls, The Professor had us rearrange the chairs (it had to be done every day) in rows facing the desk behind which she sat at the front of the room. She may have favored a Mickey Mouse T-shirt, but there was nothing Mickey Mouse about her.

Our Professor cared for each and every one of us with total equality and impartiality. She had learned all our names on the first go-around and expected us always to sit in the places we had occupied that first day. She explained some point of grammar, then handed out exercises, or wrote them on the blackboard, or on rare occasions told us to turn to one in our textbook—which was terrible, and which Claire, also, had virtually ignored. Then she asked the questions and we gave answers to them in turn.

These sessions were terrifying experiences for most of us. We were in the third month of the course, the subjunctive and the conditional were on deck, and things were getting complicated.

"Richard," The Professor would say in a stony voice, and I would strive to give the right answer. She got very angry when you gave the wrong answer, and even angrier at any student who tried to butt in with the right answer.

"Let Richard try," she would say. "*He* needs it. And *you,* don't *you* try to have more than your turn."

Then looking at me again, she would say, "Now, Richard," pronounced in French, "Ree-shar."

The Professor probed relentlessly until somehow or other you stuttered out the right answer. Her patience was as short as her temper.

"Im-be-cile," she hissed. "Idiot!" She slowly and gracefully raised her arms in the air, tilted her head back, and rolled her eyes.

"What am I to do? What *am* I to do with these unprepared people in my class?"

Then she deflated and say almost calmly, "Now, Ree-shar it is the same as Jane had." And eventually I would see.

She always went around the class in the same order, starting with the first person in the first row on her right. I always sat on the front row to the left just past center, so I could see what she wrote on the blackboard. Like everyone else, I calculated frantically which question down the line I would be asked, and tried to work out the answer before she got to it and to me. She knew we did this, but rebuked only those who tried to look up answers in dictionaries and verb books. The bad thing about it, of course, was that everyone was so desperately counting ahead and trying to prepare an answer—and working on the questions both before and after the one that was theirs, because maybe you counted wrong, and sometimes she asked you the following question, too—that no one paid much attention to the answers others gave. So what, then, if my question took an answer of the same sort as Jane had given? Likely as not I was paying no attention whatsoever to The Professor's exchange with Jane.

I had thought I was tense during some of my tutoring hours with Maya. I had not known what tense was. Or, rather, for four hours a day, five days a week, for all the days and hours of that month under The Professor's iron heel, I was more tense than I have ever been in my life or ever want to be again. The first time I ever climbed a mountain wall with hundreds of feet of exposure below me, that time we arrived back at the entrance of a cave to find a wall of water roaring in and had to crawl downstream as fast as we could for a long distance to clamber up into passages above water level, my Ph.D. oral exam—none of those times could begin to compete with the state of tension I was enduring now.

And how am I to characterize or express adequately my sensations when with every indication of justified anger and disgust, The Professor called me an idiot and an imbecile? To be sure, she called others in the class the same as the days went on, but I was the first. I, who had been a professor in charge of my own classes for twenty-five years. In some sense of that maligned word, I suppose the experience was edifying.

Once, The Professor said deliciously, "Do not have fear, Ree-shar."

It was not the first time in my life that I had been called an imbecile in class. But imbecility is in America, so to speak, a relative thing. In France, it is exactly defined, and certified.

The Professor of intensive French, Part III, taught French lycée style. It is one of the most rigid systems in the world, military in its implementation and clocklike in its precision. A French minister of education once said that if you gave him the day of the week and the hour of the day, he could tell you what every schoolchild in France was studying at that exact moment.

You are to do exactly what you are told in prescribed lengths of time, and for everything there is a rule. This is so true that the crib books available for hundreds of French university courses read like parodies of themselves. No matter what the task, from appreciating poetry to building bridges, there is a set of guidelines for proceeding, and if you memorize those guidelines and can follow them—or sometimes just reproduce them—in class, then you can be certified as a bridge builder or a poetaster.

I fear, alas, that some of this madness for rules and order stems from my hero, Descartes. In his *Discours de la Méthode* of 1637, the very book that got me into this fix in the first place, he provides a guide to life consisting of four maxims, the second of which is

> to be as firm and decisive in my actions as I could, and to follow even the most doubtful opinions, once I had adopted them, with no less constancy than if they had been quite

certain. In this respect I would be imitating a traveler who, upon finding himself lost in a forest, should not wander about turning this way and that, and still less stay in one place, but should keep walking as straight as he can in one direction, never changing it for slight reasons even if mere chance made him choose it in the first place; for in this way, even if he does not go exactly where he wishes, he will at least end up in a place where he is likely to be better off than in the middle of a forest.

Thinking like that led the English—of all people—into the disastrous Charge of the Light Brigade. The Four Hundred rode into the valley of death and died by the rules. Whenever I read Descartes's second maxim, I always have a vision of a forest a few miles wide circling the globe at the equator, and of a methodical Frenchman who wanders into it, gets lost, and then turns resolutely to march straight east.

When you are accused of a crime under the Napoleonic Code in France, you are considered guilty until proved innocent. This is just the opposite of the English and American legal systems in which the burden of proof is on the accuser, not the accused. There was a strong element of the Napoleonic Code in the instruction at the Alliance Française.

If you are told to do something by a teacher in France, you follow instructions exactly, or you are punished for it. The Professor asked us to write a page in the past tense. I did this, but my story called for a few sentences in the future tense, which I knew quite well, so I threw them in. The paper was returned with a low mark and the verbs of those sentences changed from future to past, which completely confused the sense of the text.

At the break, I went up to The Professor and said, "I meant for these to be future tense. The story doesn't make sense otherwise."

She glanced at the paper and said, "But you made mistakes. These are not past tense."

"I *meant* them to be future."

She looked at me blankly a moment, and then said a little angrily, "You made mistakes. You didn't know the past tense for these verbs."

"But I did know. I used the future on purpose."

Finally she understood what I was saying.

"Don't lie," she said. "You made mistakes."

"I am not lying," I told her in cold fury. "I know quite well the difference between future and past tenses."

The Professor was taller than I am by several inches. I am a redhead. Colleagues like to tell of how once when a taxi driver in New York City tried to overcharge us for a trip in from the airport, I got angry and so frightened him that he jumped into his taxi and drove off without being paid at all. I can't say that I remember it that way myself—he took the fare we had agreed upon at the airport—but there are a few mad Watsons—there would have to be, given how many of them became teachers—and one or another of them flies off at an acute angle now and then.

The Professor looked down at me and burst out laughing.

"But Ree-shar," she said, "if you knew they were future tense, why did you use them when I asked for the past tense?"

**A**merican students more than any others get caught by not following instructions exactly. Even with the best of intentions, it was not always easy to do an assignment correctly, because inevitably what was obvious to the French teacher was ambiguous to the foreign students. Of course learning the strictures is part of learning the language, but I was struck—as were other American teachers in the classes— by the fact that what we award students for—initiative, inventiveness, going beyond what is asked for, smart-assed showing off—is ruthlessly, even with great relish, punished in the French lycée system.

"That's right," said my friend Claude Chabert, who teaches philosophy in a lycée in Paris.

He was correcting several hundred end-of-term exams. All of them had to say the same thing.

"But then why is it that French intellectuals from Descartes to Derrida are so idiosyncratic?" I asked. "To be a French intellectual is synonymous with being an individualist."

I wondered if it was in reaction to their schooling.

"Look at Lévi-Strauss," I raved on. "He won't recognize any followers at all, they're all wrong, he says, only he can apply his method and get valid results."

Nevertheless, since 1635 when the Académie Française was established to preserve the purity of the French language, the French have obeyed the rules so faithfully that Descartes's seventeenth-century French is as easy to read as the French of today. Try reading seventeenth-century English.

I knew about French rigidity in language. But when Claire asked us to write a poem, despite my resolve not to argue with teachers about what is right in French, I found myself in dispute with her about a metaphor I had used in mine.

"You can't say that in French," she said.

"You understand what I mean?" I asked.

I had represented meaning as a thread running through a seemingly unrelated sequence of events.

"Yes," she replied. "It is perfectly clear what you mean, but you can't say that in French. That metaphor doesn't exist in French."

"But if it's perfectly clear, then why can't I introduce it?"

She looked at me in disgust. "*Maybe* if you were a great French poet you could, but *you* can't say that in French."

Later I learned that I also couldn't say that Descartes set us on the road to modern science because "on the road to" is an American idiom, not French.

Claude's brother, Jacques Chabert, who is a translator from the English and American, says there are many things that can be said in English that cannot be said in French. The greatest problem comes from English containing so many adjectives and adverbs that have only slight differences of meaning, or that do little more than give a distinctive texture in their variety to the English text, but all of which by rule must be translated by the same few French words, thus rendering a text striking in English for its richness into dull and monotonous French. Of course there are problems in the other direction, too. While translating verses for a ballet Descartes is said to have written at Queen Christina's request, I saw that alexandrines that are easy to write in

French are very difficult to render into English. It is also far easier to rhyme in French than in English.

I thought about these matters all the more as I was translating into English the French text of a small booklet about the painter Jean Truel. I argued with Claude Chabert, who wanted me to use the English cognates of three French words despite their not conveying very adequately the same meaning in English that they do in French. Eventually I let him have them. In the course of this, it came to me that the great difference between a literary tour de force in English and one in French is that a work of genius in English stretches the language as far as it will go, while genius in French literature is exhibited by superhuman adherence to the rules. Even if they have to make up the rules. Georges Perec, for example, has written a novel using only words that do not contain *e, é,* or *è,* which you would think would be impossible to do in French, but he did it. Probably I should be pictured here with a lightbulb lighting up over my head to show my sudden understanding of what must be a commonplace observation. It is the French and not the Germans after all who are rule bound (at least in language). This opened to me the dark possibility that although I like to read French, perhaps I don't really like French.

One can so easily parody The Professor with her Mickey Mouse T-shirt—which, incidentally, she never wore again, and which contrasted strikingly with the severe suits and blouses she wore during the rest of the term—but she *was* a professor. She was given the most trouble, as were all the

Alliance Française teachers, by American secondary school teachers taking the course for summer school credit. The Americans disputed constantly with the French teachers about how the courses were being taught. They didn't like Claire's prima donna performances, they hated The Professor's rigidity, and they fumed at the haphazard approach of the teacher who taught Part IV. I argued with these American teachers that we simply had to go along with it, whatever it was, as most of the other foreign students did. The main point was, after all, just to be there, to force oneself to be in class four hours a day, five days a week, speaking and listening to French. How it was presented was incidental.

"Did it ever occur to you," one of them snapped at me, "that you might be doing better yourself if the teacher were any good?"

At the Alliance Française, the American secondary school teachers were enraged at the use of unfocusable overhead projectors for displaying exercises on a screen. To make the print (or handwriting) large enough, the teacher always had to show the page only partially, often with the beginnings or endings of sentences cut off. Every time the teacher advanced the page, students groaned that they hadn't finished the previous part.

"Too bad," the teacher would say. "There has been plenty of time."

I think the French must have invented the overhead projector.

One day while I was standing in line at the American Express in Paris to cash a check, an American engineer told me his problems. (A Frenchman would not have spoken to a stranger.) This engineer had come to Paris at the urgent request of a French company to show them some new equipment his company had designed.

"We make things on the KISS principle," he said. "You know, Keep It Simple, Stupid. This equipment is nearly foolproof. The French decided they didn't want it. You know what they said? It wasn't complicated enough!"

I told him of a game I had invented. It came to me while I was learning the French "lost thread" method of surveying caves, which involves using a box in which a spool of thread unwinds over a measuring wheel as you walk from one survey point to the next. At each survey point you read off the distance, snip off the thread (losing it), tie the loose end onto a projection, and march on to the next survey point.

My new game is called French Engineering. You set a problem—for example, eliminating dog shit from the sidewalks of Paris. This is, by the way, a massive problem. I recall reading somewhere that four hundred tons appear on the streets each day, which seems a lot, but perhaps not if you remember that no French family or shop is complete without a dog—and some of those dogs are *big*. Little children in Paris are taught not only to look both ways before crossing the street, but also to look down before walking on the sidewalk.

But back to the game. The problem is set. Everyone works out an engineering solution, and then, of course, the most complicated design wins. In the actual case of dog shit, the municipal engineers win. To rid the sidewalks of dog shit, the City of Paris utilizes an apparatus that is bolted around a very large motorcycle—not just a motor scooter, but a big, heavy hog that could probably do sixty miles an hour from a dead stop in six seconds. The apparatus consists of a large vacuum cleaner snout on each side of the front wheel with hoses four inches in diameter leading back to large containers surrounding the back wheel. The operator, a young man or woman in a distinctive green uniform, rides this machine rapidly down the sidewalk, weaving among pedestrians, to stop with the front wheel properly positioned beside each pile of dog shit, left or right, that they come across. The appropriate snout is lowered over the mess, the motorcycle engine is raced, the dog shit is vacuumed into the back container, a spray of water is released, and the spot is cleaned.

Theoretically.

In fact, the spot is usually left shit slippery, and as the cyclist races on to the next prize, bits of dog shit dribble from the snouts. Granted that large quantities of dog shit are removed this way, another result is that small quantities are more evenly distributed on the sidewalks. These shreds are more difficult to avoid than the tidy displays the dogs themselves deposit.

London has a dog shit problem, too, but the solution of the municipality there, as might be expected, earns virtually no points at all in the game of French Engineering. In fact, you might fault the Brits for not following the rules, because we assumed that the game demanded a technological solution, didn't we? The English, in their typical muddling way, introduced not a mechanical solution, but rather one in social engineering. A fine was levied of twenty pounds (about thirty-five dollars) for anyone whose dog defecated on the sidewalk, and the law was enforced. Now London's sidewalks, once as hazardous as those in Paris to shoe leather and good spirits—for nothing is so instantly mood altering as stepping in dog shit—are virtually clean. Well, clean of dog shit, anyway. I have heard that the City Fathers of Paris invited Mayor Koch of New York City for consultation after New York passed its pooper-scooper law, but if this libelous rumor is true, it is clear that the French rejected the socio-legal solution as unfair.

Besides being patrolled by shit-eating motorcycles, Parisian streets—does this count in the game?—are washed every morning with water that wells up out of the gutters and is swept along with whatever debris is in the way by men with brooms; in addition, the sidewalks are often washed by water sprayed from a variety of vehicles that defy succinct description. I might, however, say a word about the brooms. At first you think, "How quaint, they still use willow-twig brooms," but on closer examination you see that the bundles of twigs tied on the ends of long sticks are actually made of brown plastic in a variety of branchings to replicate exactly the shapes of twigs. The French win hands down.

The rebellious American school teachers did their arithmetic in front of the Alliance Française teachers. Twenty-five students at $300 a head amounts to $7,500 for one month's tuition, unrefundable. They doubted seriously that the teacher earned more than $1,000 or $1,500 a month for teaching a class (no teacher would ever tell), so the school could at the very least damned well provide copies of all exercises for all students. And throw the overhead projectors into the Seine.

There was one copy machine at the Alliance Française for some one hundred and thirty teachers, with, in the French way, its own operator, who, in the French way, worked at his own speed when he felt like it. But there was no point in blaming him, because the machine was almost always out of order. Consequently, teachers wanting to provide copies of exercises for students would have to pay for them out of their own pockets, at street rates of seventeen cents a page. Not bloody likely.

Outside class, I talked French mostly to Claude Chabert, lycée teacher of philosophy and (I have his word) France's premier cave explorer (as of the hour and day, and perhaps even the week, that he considered the question). Claude is editing a who's who of French cavers, ranked according to exploit and reputation.

"Why don't you do one for American cavers?" he asked.

"I couldn't imagine it," I said.

But climbers are ranked in America, I thought, why not cavers?

"We know who is good and doing things," I said to the French caver whom Claude later sent to me.

She was writing a general survey of world caving.

"Can you give me the names of the major American cavers and what they are doing?" she asked. "And their birth dates?"

"Not really," I said, trying not to laugh. She was very serious.

Claude's patience in letting me take time to think how to say what I had in mind was gratifying after a day in class where the teacher admonished continually, "Don't think! Say it." I knew I must reach that point, and I envied the young students who could instantly repeat back set phrases, and then continue with tense and number modulations appropriate to a continuing conversation. I could do it, because I knew the grammar, if I was given time to think. Claude listened, corrected the essentials, and with him I learned to talk.

Some French people merely listened and never questioned my French except when they could make nothing at all of it. Others, like Michel Siffre (France's premier cave scientist, as distinguished from cave explorer), were stern pedagogues. Sometimes when talking to Michel I would forget what I was trying to say as I strove to integrate his corrections into my speech. The necessity to ignore the corrections and go on if I were to keep my arguments in mind also helped me to learn to talk. By the end of the second month at the Alliance Française, I still had trouble bringing up common words that I knew perfectly well, but I could talk to any individual Frenchman. Mostly, however, only to individuals. If a Frenchman was trapped alone with me—I tried to set up luncheon engagements with individual Cartesian scholars—he understood all I said and we could talk about anything. In groups, the French had no patience and refused to understand me.

"Vous . . . ," I would start to say. ("You . . . ," pronounced *voo*.)

"Quoi?" the Frenchman would reply. ("What?")

"Vous . . ."
"Quoi?"
"*Vous!*"
"Ah!" A great light transforms his facial features. "*Vous.*"

It is time seriously to consider whether or not I had or have some internal resistance to learning to speak French. After all, my brother speaks fluent Cantonese and Mandarin. My daughter, Anna, is fluent in German and Japanese and is mistaken for a Parisian when she speaks French. My wife, Pat, . . . but she is not a blood relation, never mind her half a dozen languages. I can make all the sounds, so why is learning so slow?

I have mentioned a possible psychological reason. Although I loved learning to read French and enjoy reading French philosophers and writers, I have a distinct dislike for the sound of spoken French. Many Americans do. Why? Because it's weak. For American men at least, French sounds syrupy and effeminate. This came home to me in class when the teacher of Part IV played a tape of a poem by Jacques Prévert, a French poet loved and renowned for writing simple poems about simple things. All of my teachers at the Alliance Française used and praised his poems. To give you a proper sense of them, let me say that once in class when the teacher went around the room to have each of us give our impressions of a poem by Prévert, I commented that Prévert is the perfect poet for sentimental adolescents. The teacher and the adolescents in class protested, but another American, a woman of a certain age, defended my view.

The poem played on tape was about how to paint a bird. First you paint a cage, then you paint flowers and plants around it, a beautiful sky, and so on. You wait. Your painting is bad if a bird doesn't come and land in the cage. If one does, it is good and you can erase the cage and sign your name to the painting of the bird. Putting aside the cuteness of all this, what made me realize how much I disliked the sound of French was the continual, unctuous, caressing repetition of "l'oiseau" ("the bird"). It is a word the French believe to be one of the most beautiful in their language. It is a word that cannot be pronounced without simpering, a word whose use should be restricted to children under five.

I did not want to speak French because it gave me the bird.

Of course I agree with you totally that this is an absurd reaction—to the sound of "l'oiseau," but not, let me hasten to add, to Prévert's poetry, which is detestable in any language.

So how does one handle such an irrational response? I wondered if it was just the contrast with the English "bird," which is a strong hard word. How about the German word for bird, "Vogel"? I'm going to get to German in a moment. American men don't like to simper. And as I said, they get their notion of Frenchmen from the movies. Certainly no American boy of my generation ever wanted to grow up to be Charles Boyer.

The French can't even swear properly. This is where the Germans come in. Germans say "Verdammte!" and "Gott im Himmel!" and we say "God damn!" and what do the French say?

"Mon Dieu!"

Notice the gutturals in the English and German. You can really curse with *g* and *d*. And you might think "Mon Dieu!" could be half saved with the *d*, but no chance, for you must emasculate it by sliding up into the French *u* sound, which requires you to purse your lips and point them up at a forty-five degree angle to make that high *ew* sound that exists in practically no other language but French. It is the *ew* of "ew, la, la" made by a little English girl with a twist in her body, the edge of her skirt held up between thumb and index finger, her head tilted, her eyes half closed and glazed, to represent someone (that's right, a French someone) who thinks herself most hoity-toity—which itself comes surely from the French for high roof . . . In plain English, it is embarrassing for an American to pronounce the French *u* because the mere sound of it suggests that the speaker thinks very highly of himself or herself, "ew . . . dew tell . . ."

All right. All right. But remember, I'm not trying to be reasonable about it. I'm just giving you my unadulterated, stupid, automatic response. Real Men Don't Speak French. There has to be something to that. Where did I read that during World War I, French soldiers were known as "Wee-wees"? Of course that's French for "Yes, yes," but really . . .

There was also World War II.

"What would you ever want to go there for?" the TWA clerk asked me. He was big, gruff, and efficient, in his early sixties. Just enough older than me.

"You'd never catch me going there," he said, pounding the stapler with a meaty fist. "Wouldn't even fight for their own country!" He glared at me as he handed over my ticket. "Have a nice day."

During this monologue I had a sickly grin on my face. In 1941, I was ten years old. In 1941, I reckon he was eighteen.

My uncle Harold Watson (a teacher) was gassed by the Germans in France during World War I, and my uncle Harold Penwell (a teacher) walked across a lot of fields in Germany and France during World War II, and both of them said to me, "Germans were so much like us that we wondered why we were fighting them and not the damned frogs."

French cave explorers, I told Claire's class when I gave my presentation, are the toughest and most macho in the world. For example, the American technique for ascending a single rope involves use of a mechanical ascender into which you insert both feet. Then you climb up the rope by pushing down with both legs, step after step, like an inchworm. The French system, however, involves the use of an ascender with which you push yourself up the rope using only one leg, the other elegantly dangling free. The Frenchman, therefore, ostentatiously climbs the rope with only half his available leg power. There are other significant examples, but I used as my culminating argument the following. Americans generally favor low leather boots for exploring caves, boots that in a short time have their toes worn off from dragging them when one crawls on rock and sand. When you wade, your feet do get wet, but when you get back on dry ground, the water runs out the open toes and eventually your boots and feet dry out. On the contrary, the French always wear high rubber boots that come nearly up to their knees. French cavers are careful never to crawl, so they do not wear holes in the toes of their boots. When they wade in deep water, as they always do, their high rubber boots fill with cold water, which they never dump out. Consequently, not only do French cavers always carry several kilos of water in their boots, but also they are always walking in cold water, and this is why among cave explorers they are the toughest and most macho in the world.

Claire said, "You speak English using French words."

I was a pretty good caver myself, once. But then my eyes and knees began to play tricks on me. I fancy I could have learned to speak French once, too, with a flair, back when the muscle in my brain was limber.

Anyway, that TWA clerk probably missed *Casablanca,* that scene where Humphrey Bogart gives up Ingrid Bergman to go off with Claude Rains to win the war. Now there was a real Frenchman . . .

Having been a college professor for a quarter of a century in the course of which I have become inured to making a fool of myself, I would like to think that these cultural and linguistic prejudices—which I readily admit having—nevertheless do not impede me from learning to speak French. I screw up my face and pronounce my *u*'s like a Frenchman, and no Frenchman is going to think I'm not macho because of it. I suspect there is a more serious, structural impediment. Claude noticed it at once, and Claire had commented on it.

"You speak in French words," Claude granted me, "but you arrange them mostly in English sentences."

Nicky—she has lived with Claude for fifteen years, or perhaps it is the other way around—often straightened out the words for me. Besides rearranging your words, the French also substitute phrases. To speak (and write) French, you have not only first to use French words, and second to arrange them in French sentence forms, but also you have to use French clichés (and, as I learned with my poem, *only* French clichés).

This is commonplace. To speak and write French, you have to think like a Frenchman. Why not?

Why did I resist it so? Because, I think, all my life I have been trying to learn to write. These new French forms threatened to destroy what little progress I had made so far. Not only did I use English forms in speaking French, I was appalled to find myself using French forms when I was writing English. French was undermining my very being! My personality was in danger of disintegrating! A great clanging of alarm bells was set off in my deep unconscious, irritated by these alien influences seeping down from above.

"You try to say too complicated things," Claude said. "Just say simple things."

Claude would do anything to win an argument.

By letting it all hang out, to use a cliché that won't go in French, letting the apparent source of my rejection of French forms stand out in all its ridiculous vainglory, did I manage to be mature and put my childish fears aside? No. But I now understood two things from within. The first was what Milan Kundera means when he talks of the extermination of an indigenous literature. If, for whatever reason, one cannot think, talk, and write Czech without interference, then this is the death of Czech language and literature. It comes from a feeling of cultural or national insignificance. It comes from having to learn an official language such as German or Russian in which all "important" transactions must be conducted. The threat could be felt by any foreign writer who cares to sit for a while in French classes at the Alliance Française in Paris under the iron rule of teachers who believe as much as did Corneille and Racine that French not only is the language of God but also is the only language in which human beings can say with crystal clarity exactly what they mean.

In the front of the latest book by Kundera, Czechoslavakia's greatest living writer, the publisher notes that Kundera, who had lived in Paris for some years at the behest of Russian-speaking officials in Prague, wrote it in French.

And a dog can learn to dance on two hind legs.

The other thing I understood is why many writers resist learning a foreign language. They are defending the style and form they have perfected in their own language.

The mere reading of another language apparently does not present the same threat. But speaking is too close to writing.

In any event, my job was to get on with learning to speak French. One problem was that there are so many French words that are spelled differently, and mean different things, but are pronounced the same, far more than is the case in English. There is even a standard book—for *French* students of French—of a couple of hundred pages that contains nothing but lists of words that sound alike. This gives rise to an excruciating kind of torture in the French elementary school system that is almost unheard of in America except in secretarial schools for learning shorthand. This is the "dictée," or dictation. French children have dictation almost every school day up to the age of fifteen, and dictations are a popular contest for adults on French television.

I had never taken a dictation before entering the Alliance Française, and then only two weeks before the end of the course when the teacher began giving them to us every day in preparation for the final exam. Dictation was not new to students who had taken French in Germany, Spain, or other European countries, but it was new to most of the Americans.

I do not spell well in English, again perhaps a function of reading for meaning, not for the sound of the words nor for how they look on the page. I spell even worse in French. (Now that I've worked at learning to spell French words, I spell English words even worse than before.) On dictations I always made about twice as many errors as the number the teacher announced as allowable. I began to worry about passing the dictation portion of the final exam, and, like the other American school teachers, began fuming about how the course was taught.

My mood was not improved by an article my mother sent me from the *Des Moines Sunday Register* by Stanley Meisler titled "The Dreaded Dictée: French Learning Game." Under the dateline "Paris, France," he begins:

Once a day, children in France's elementary schools take the dictée—several nerve-wracking, sometimes dreaded minutes in which they must write down exactly what their teacher dictates to them. It is as French as frog legs and Calvados and the Eiffel Tower, and nothing reveals all that is unique in the French educational system better than the dictée.

The dictée tests spelling and grammar and, as usually graded, demands near perfection. A few errors mean failure, even a zero. It sometimes seems that nothing is more important in French education.

Americans, of course, have spelling bees. But a spelling bee bears about as much resemblance to the dictée as chopped liver does to foie gras. A spelling bee is simply not as intricate or fearsome or significant.

If it was so infernally important, why hadn't we been having dictation every day at the Alliance Française?

In the philosophy courses I teach, there have been over the years a number of older students, forty, fifty, sixty years old, working on a degree again or for the first time. They work hard and usually pass. They are always anxious, and I reassure them.

"You can learn just as easily now as when you were twenty," I say. "Relax. Don't worry. Just read the material and do the work. Many of the kids don't, you know. You'll do fine."

But now I began to wonder if I knew what I was talking about. At the Alliance Française, I sank lower and lower to the bottom of the class. I never missed a session. I sat there paying intense attention and looking at the teacher with hopeful eyes.

My transition to this groveling state of supplication was abrupt. During that first month with Claire, I was often impatient. I was used to being in charge and had consciously to hold myself down so as not to behave like a professor, not to speak up on all subjects like a know-it-all. I did know many things the younger students did not on subjects that came up in class discussion. But this problem evaporated like dew under the desert sun during the first hour with The Professor. By the end of the first day with her I was so anxious simply to be able to work out the exercises and answer the questions in class that I lost consciousness of ever having been a professor—or of knowing anything—at all. In The Professor's class I saw myself as did the youngest members—as a funny little old man with a white beard who was earnest and wanted to learn but who just wasn't very good or very bright. They liked me and would talk to me at break, but there was no question who was at the bottom of the class. Actually, the absolute bottom was a very nice Austrian boy who never studied, never knew an answer, and also never missed a class. I have often had students like him in my own classes. They seldom give any evidence of being either bored or stupid. They just don't do any work, and they never complain when they fail. Why are they there? To be, I suppose, a member of the group.

I try to find some way to answer the question of whether or not students are tense or even terrified in the classes I teach, as I was that second month at the Alliance Française. If so, I have been largely blind to it.

The Professor knew that many of her students were trembling, and she exploited it. I thought at first that she doted on her power to exterminate us, but later I was sure that this was not true at all. It is the way many teachers in France teach. They are, after all, in charge.

I said this to Madame Elisabeth Labrousse, a grand old scholar who works on skepticism, Pierre Bayle, and French Protestantism. She has on her wall a wonderful seventeenth-century print depicting the ages of man, the last of which translates into English as something like "driviality."

After I had told my sad tale, she laughed and laughed, and in turn told me this story: "My apartment backs onto a schoolyard for the primary grades. One day I heard through my open kitchen window the most awful language. I looked out, and there with his back to me was a professor, raging and swearing at the top of his voice at a group of twenty or thirty little children, standing in rows. They could not help but see me and so after a moment, I put my thumbs in my ears and waggled my fingers at them. They shrieked with laughter and their professor got all the angrier. I stepped back before he could turn to see me. But isn't it wonderful? Those little children, only seven and eight years old, already so relaxed in such a situation."

I just hadn't had the proper upbringing. Otherwise I would not be so tense. Would that someone had thumbed her ears at me. But, no, it wouldn't have done any good. I was strung up very tight. I thought of Bill Gus, a Greek who worked in the Sheffield Brick and Tile Plant where I worked summers when I was an undergraduate in college.

He surely had not been christened Bill, or even William, and his last name had obviously been shortened. He was forty or sixty years old (I never thought of it then, and thinking back now I haven't a clue), and he could not speak English. He could swear, and put a number of English words together in such a way that you could, once you got used to his accent, understand what he wanted to say. He used to go into rages when people did not understand him, which was often, and which led some of his co-workers to pretend not to understand when they really did, just to set him off. He knew or suspected this, which made him even more furious.

I know exactly how he felt. The owner of the brickyard was a second-generation Greek American who had made good on a deposit of Iowa clay, a variety of dirt the farmers had little use for. He dug it up, made drainage tile out of it, and sold it to the farmers to bury again. Some said through generosity, others said through avarice because they came cheap, he recruited some of his laborers in Greece. Bill Gus was one who could never save enough to go back. He was said sometimes on Saturday night drunks to break down and cry about a wife and children he had left behind. He was sixty or eighty when someone finally paid his way back to Greece. No one in Sheffield ever heard of him again.

Pat and I lived in Greece for a year once, and you know, that is one hard language. Even Pat had trouble with it.

I was determined to learn to speak French.

In Don DeLillo's novel *White Noise,* there is an American professor who establishes a Center for Hitler Studies. He and it become rather distinguished, and much of the tension and humor of one of the subplots of the novel depends upon the hairbreadth escapes of this American scholar as he organizes, presides over, and triumphs at an International Hitler Studies Conference without once revealing that he can neither read nor write nor speak German.

How many years had I been a Cartesian scholar when I read that novel? Many. There I was, reading and comprehending the most complicated French constructions, even publishing translations from the French. Yet in that peculiar and pathetic way of so many American scholars, I had only the most rudimentary, effectively nonexistent ability to write and speak the language in which the books that formed the body of my scholarly research and reputation were written.

I had been, as I protested to my mother, always too busy to learn. But when you got right down to it, the true answer was simply that it had never been worth the trouble.

But how could one be a Cartesian scholar, even have something of a reputation, if one did not speak French? The answer is plain: Only in America. Only in the American academic world could it make no difference one way or another whether a Cartesian scholar spoke French. Or, for that matter, whether a Kantian scholar spoke German. It is possible in America to have a reputation as a Cartesian or Kantian scholar without even being able to *read* French or German. I did know a few people in that tight and special circle of French Cartesian scholars that revolved around the Sorbonne, but the exclusiveness of that world was such that it was of no particular advantage for me actually to talk to them. As long as my career was in American academe, I could get all I needed from the French by reading their books.

Once I decided to learn to speak French it became—did I say?—almost immediately an obsession. All those years of guilt and embarrassment at being a Cartesian scholar who could not speak French (even if no one else noticed or cared), the difference between what I was and what I appeared to be, combined to drive my ambition to a frenzy. I would learn to speak French, whatever it took, however long. One day, by God, I would sit at a table in a restaurant in Paris with a group of French Cartesian scholars, and we would talk!

After you have been a teacher for a while, it is very difficult to be a student. Those American secondary school teachers at the Alliance Française were swollen with suppressed authority. Their very tone of voice indicated that they resented not being in charge of the class. They knew perfectly well that they could run it better than any of our teachers. Our French teachers bristled, and rushed to put down the rebellions.

Once when one of the American school teachers had completed a routine exercise correctly, The Professor said with great hoked-up enthusiasm, "That's right, Jane! Wonderful! That was very good. Excellent!" Then she said dryly, "That's an example of teaching by the American system."

At the break I argued with Jane that everyone said the Alliance Française teachers were a real grab bag, and she could get someone a lot worse than The Professor. She went to the main office and transferred to another section, anyway. One of the features of the size and basic anonymity of the

Alliance Française is that I never saw her again, so I don't know how she fared.

The Professor's joke on Jane precipitated a small revolt, the result of which was that three other American school teachers transferred out of the class. The next day The Professor announced that she had been accused of being too strict, and that several students had transferred to other sections. Any of us could do the same if we wished. Then she went around the class individually.

"Ree-shar, do you want to transfer?"

"No, no," I said in a rush. "I like strict."

She laughed mirthlessly, as though she now knew what perversion I preferred. Under direct inquiry, none of the other students wanted to transfer. The Professor thereafter was, if anything, meaner than before.

I disliked intensely not being in charge. Nevertheless, I was prepared to suffer student status, to let the teacher be center stage and call all the shots. I would do what I was told. But just as I had quit exploring caves about the time my old joints told me it was time to quit, I now noticed that the hinges of my brain had rusted, and possibly under strain some parts had broken off and were flapping loose.

No! I would not quit.

I took up jogging in my early thirties and soon learned that if I could not run faster than younger men, I could often run longer. One thing caving and aging had given me was endurance. So while those young pups in my class went to cafés at night, made love, and lived the life of Parisians, I studied all the time. The problem was that the race was for the swift, not the strong. Alice's millipede couldn't walk when he stopped to think about it. I couldn't talk unless I did. The younger students stepped right out without the slightest pause, conjugating, say, reflexive verbs with "être" rather than with "avoir," a rule I knew quite well but could not apply as they did off the tops of their heads, but only after looking inside my own.

Babies can more easily keep their balance by learning to run before they learn to walk. We talk before we have conscious knowledge of grammar. I was going at it the wrong way. I had to bury my knowledge of the rules in my unconscious before I could talk. You don't learn to ride a bicycle out of a book. You have to embody the rules and let them operate without thought. I knew all that.

"Don't you just want to rub your hands on their fuzzy heads?"

It was not Claire saying this flirtatiously, but our severe Professor standing in front of an unbelieving American girl who was sitting beside a North African black.

"I always do," The Professor said deliciously, making a pass with both her hands as though she were going to. The black guy grinned and ducked.

The teachers told ethnic jokes. Here is the best one: One Jew visits another who runs a Kosher restaurant. They talk in the kitchen where the Chinese dishwasher joins in their conversation in Yiddish. As the guy leaves he says to his friend, "How amazing. That's the first Chinese I ever saw who could speak Yiddish." "Keep your voice down," the restaurant owner said. "He thinks I'm teaching him French."

None of the professors corrected our accents except on rare occasions when they really couldn't understand. They couldn't do everything, but they did occasionally counsel a student to take a special class in pronunciation.

"In my experience," The Professor said, "only Germans and Poles can learn to speak French without an accent. The Italians and the Spanish are the worst. A native Spanish speaker can never get rid of a heavy accent."

The most annoying? "The Spanish. Almost intolerable."

Wasn't the American bad? "No, Americans can never lose their accent, but it's not particularly annoying."

"The most charming accent is the Irish," she said, beaming at Higgins, one of only two class members older than me during the three months. At first she called him "Père Higgins," pronounced "Per'iggins," which was pretty cute in itself.

One day when we went around the room answering a question asked by the student on our left and asking a question of the one on our right, I asked Higgins why The Professor called him "Père" ("Father"). Was he a priest?

"No," he said. "I belong to a teaching brotherhood, and she probably calls me 'Père' because in the photograph on my Alliance Française identity card I'm wearing a clerical collar."

The Professor said that I had asked a good question and that he had given a good answer. Henceforth she called him "Frèr'iggins" ("Brother Higgins").

My question was partly curiosity but also was motivated by indignation. Had the French Enlightenment taken place for naught? She called what she took to be a man of the cloth "Père" and then "Frère," but me she called not "Professeur," but "Ree-shar." The last priest has yet to be strangled with the intestines of the last lawyer in France.

Any foreigner who has been in France tells stories of how nasty the French are, and travelers' books about France are full of them. They are all true, but largely misinterpreted. The French are a private people, and most of their business is none of yours. You interrupt their lives and hurt their ears by mangling the greatest glory of France, its language, and they are both insulted and, to put it bluntly, not interested. They simply do not care who you are, what you are doing, or what you want. This is, for Americans in particular, difficult to understand. Americans are always interested in what other people are doing, and they find their own affairs fascinating. They talk to people on the street, they tell strangers their intimate secrets on trains, and they make lifelong friends on trans-Atlantic flights. You speak to a Frenchman and likely as not he will simply turn away. If he can't leave, he will ignore you.

The supreme example of this that I have observed was a scene that took place in a park in central Paris. Along with a number of other people I was sitting at a table in a restaurant bordering the park, eating lunch. People were strolling along. I soon noticed that in the park, a hundred feet away, under a tree, an attractive young couple were being more affectionate than is usual in public. Being an American, interested in what other people do, I gaped for a few moments, but then I realized that this young couple, who were engaged in what is, after all, a rather commonplace activity, were far from what was most interesting about the scene. Practically no one except a few foreigners like me had deigned to notice what was going on. Not the French people sitting at tables in the restaurant with, so to speak, box office seats. Not the French people strolling by. And now, in fact, not even me. I was much more interested in watching the nonwatchers than the nonwatched. True, the young couple did not appear to be French. But I don't think that it would have mattered if they were. They were ignored not out of the disdain accorded to foreigners who don't know how to behave. They were ignored because the French are not interested in what other people do.

This might explain why some French anthropologists who study the ways of life of other people sometimes seem in the books they write about them to be impatiently annoyed. It was an imposition on the Frenchman to have had to notice.

I was exposed to French nastiness when I was young and resilient, and rather liked the challenge. Anyone who pays attention can see that the French are just as nasty to one another as they are to foreigners. This goes a long way toward absolving them of the accusation that they are picking on you. They don't notice that it *is* you. To be sure, this phenomenon is more pronounced in Paris than in the provinces, but for most foreigners—for most Parisians and, as far as that goes, for most of the French—Paris is

France. Even outside Paris, any French man or woman in a position of authority, and especially those in the government bureaucracy, is duty bound to be aloof, rigid, and severe. Most annoying to Americans is the almost universal refusal of clerks and shopkeepers to help you. If they don't have what you want, or cannot figure out instantly what it is you want, they dismiss you. No, they have no idea where you might find another pharmacy, and they angrily give you to understand that if they don't have aspirin, probably it does not exist.

Michel Siffre, whom Pat and I have always suspected of being Italian because he is so nice, remarked that a crucial scene in my novel *The Runner* would be incomprehensible to most French readers. The hero goes into The Athlete's Foot and a nice young woman helps him try on almost every running shoe in the store before he finds the pair he wants.

"In France," Michel says, "he would have been thrown out after trying on the second pair." Actually, Michel said "the first pair," but surely he was exaggerating.

One evening early in World War II, just after dark, there came a furtive tapping on the door of Pastor André Trocmé's house in the small village of Chambon-sur-Lignon in the beautiful Massif Central province of rural France. Pastor Trocmé's wife opened the door, and a young woman asked quickly if she could come in. A stranger. Pastor Trocmé's wife let her in and closed the door. The young woman was a Jew. That was the beginning of a rescue operation that involved the entire village and the surrounding countryside. During the course of the war, thousands of Jews were smuggled through Chambon-sur-Lignon on their way to Switzerland, or were housed and protected in the village and on the surrounding farms. Many Jewish children were kept in the area all through the war. The Vichy French officials who worked for the Nazis knew what was going on, but whenever they raided, warnings had come in from the surrounding area, and the Jews were hidden. The fascists once found a group of young children and took them away. Rather than letting them go alone, Pastor Trocmé's brother Daniel went with them. He and they all died in the Majdanek Camp.

Forty years later Pat and I lived just outside Chambon-sur-Lignon while our daughter, Anna, went to school at Collège Cévenol there. And were the French any nicer in Chambon-sur-Lignon than elsewhere in France? Not particularly.

After the war, an interviewer persistently asked Pastor Trocmé why they had let the woman in? Why did they do it?

Pastor Trocmé answered angrily that when someone asks for help, you give it.

The rescue operation at Chambon-sur-Lignon was unique in all of France. Why? Philip Hallie, who has written a book about it, thinks it is because the people of Chambon-sur-Lignon and the surrounding area are Protestants. They are descendants of the Huguenots who were much persecuted in France, which is predominantly Catholic. Several hundred thousand Huguenots left France during the seventeenth century in search of religious freedom, but they would not have been murdered had they stayed. In the twentieth century, in France, the Jews had no choice.

Not all Parisians are nasty, of course. Pat and I have never been made so warmly members of a group as we were by the Spéléo Club de Paris. Once, when I was showing slides and got one in sideways, rather than taking it out and putting it in correctly, I simply picked up the projector and turned it sideways, which worked fine with my own crude American projector at home. The French projector, however, came apart in my hands and all its pieces fell on the floor. Those happy French cavers just laughed, and some twenty minutes later after they had it put back together again, one of them even cheerfully offered to run the projector for me during the rest of my presentation. Truly, some of my best friends are French cavers.

"Why," I asked Claude, "are all the French cavers so friendly with us, but most French scholars are not? We are just as well known in our professions as we are as cavers." I had not been successful in arranging meetings with French Cartesian scholars.

"I will think about it," Claude said.

The next day he said, "It is because the scholars are professionals. The cavers are not."

It is true that in the whole world there is no one more professional than a professor in a French university. But there has to be more to it than that. In fact, scholars in other countries are not so exclusive as the French. In Sweden, they are so helpful that they do your research for you. You read a paper in Holland at one university and people from two others come up and ask you to read a paper at theirs. In London they invite you to stay in their homes, they tell you about lectures and seminars that you might be interested in, and they invite you to contribute chapters to books. There is this little world of strange people interested in the most obscure things, and among these people camaraderie arises, if for no other reason, perhaps, than because there are so few of them. They don't often run into people who are as nutty as they are. In France, they don't want to.

Scholars compete for prestige, and each scholar—particularly each and every idiosyncratic French scholar—attempts to make dominant his own views and interpretations. In no place in the world is this competition more intense than in Paris, the intellectual capital of the Western world. Those tight little circles of the sort I was yearning just to look into were closed not through any particularly conscious intent, but because competition is so extreme among the small number who must be admitted that they haven't time to notice outsiders. Even more, in their assurance that the French intellectual circles are indeed the highest in the cosmos—a conviction they hold without ever thinking about it, as other people take for granted the air they breathe—French scholars can ignore the work of foreigners as having no relevance to them. Even French scientists seldom make reference to work in languages other than French. Another reason, of course, is that many of them can read only French.

There is actually something of this in French caving. There has never been any possibility of the French translating and publishing *The Longest Cave,* which is about Mammoth Cave in Kentucky. Most French cavers couldn't care less about caves outside France. They are willing to show you theirs, but they don't want to see yours.

And that insight gave me the clue I needed. The little circle of Parisian Cartesian scholars is the hardest to crack because Descartes *is* France, as all Frenchmen who glance without pause at the title of a recent book, *Descartes c'est la France,* know.

What in God's name is a foreigner—and not even a European at that—doing setting himself up as a Cartesian scholar? Particularly when he can't even speak the language of Descartes.

The French tell this story. A student at the Sorbonne turned in his dissertation to his major professor, who said, "Give me your phone number. I'll get back to you in about ten days." Months went by and the student heard nothing, so he tried phoning the professor. He was never home. The student went to the professor's office. He was never in his office. When the student tried to catch him at a lecture, the lecture had been canceled. Then the professor went on leave for a year. Of course the student did not spend every hour of every day trying to locate his professor. The young man had a job, he had to earn a living, he got married, he had begun a family. Twelve years went by. Then one day, not hoping for anything, he walked by the professor's office. The door was open and there the professor sat, a stack of papers on his desk in front of him. The student stepped trembling into the room and asked about his dissertation.

"Oh yes," his professor said smiling brightly. "I know right where it is." He laid his hand firmly on the mound of paper on his desk. "Give me your phone number. I'll get back to you in about ten days."

**I** had not yet managed to make an appointment with a French Cartesian scholar. Madame Rodis-Lewis would certainly have talked to me, but she was out of town.

The French may be the only people in the world who are not delighted when a foreigner tries to speak their language. Say a few halting words in Turkish to a Turk in Turkey and you will melt right through the ice of one of the most fiercely xenophobic people on earth. I was reminded of this at the Alliance Française when I spoke a few remembered words to a Turkish student in my class. He thereafter tried to speak Turkish to me at every break until I convinced him that we should speak French because that was what we were there to learn.

The peoples of every other land will make every effort to understand what you want to say, but the French go out of their way not to understand you. I reject the exceptions (some of my best friends) and the mealymouthed ameliorization that has resulted from De Gaulle's having finally reached the brains of this nation of shopkeepers with his pronouncement that if you want to fleece the tourists, you have to pay some attention to their bleating.

My daughter, Anna, who knows them both well says the Japanese are in fact worse than the French. She told me the story of an Englishman, fluent in Japanese, who trekked across northern Japan on his own. Once, stopping for the night in a village inn, he was told to move on, because they could not give him a bed or feed him.

"But I can see that you have beds and food," he said, "and I have money to pay."

"No," they said firmly, "it is impossible."

"But why?"

"Because," they said, "you don't speak Japanese, so we don't know what you want."

"But we are *speaking* Japanese," he said in great exasperation, "and you know exactly what I want. You said it. A bed and food."

This caused them some consternation, but after they consulted with one another, their spokesman said, "No, it is impossible. You cannot speak Japanese because you are not Japanese. So we cannot understand you. Please, now, be so kind as to go to the next village, where there might be someone who knows your barbaric language, and will understand that you want food and a bed for the night."

I'll bet that story was first told about the French.

One day the door opened in The Professor's class at the Alliance Française. Claire—who had told us she would be doing administration this month—stepped in and said she was counting numbers of students. She immediately picked out her old students and asked us by name how we were doing—and thereby introduced an ambience into the room entirely different from that The Professor had established. Claire, like many people, defined her job in terms of personal relationships. The Professor, on the other hand, kept her relations to us strictly professional. Claire projected her personality into and through her job, always engaging her students with her full self and ego. When she slumped down in relaxation at the end of a class day, students inquired how things were going with the man she was living with, with whom she had been so exasperated the day before.

It would have been inconceivable to inquire into the personal life of The Professor. What brightened her up were the vagaries of irregular verbs and the little oddities of usage that have no conceivable rationale or purpose except for detecting German spies who otherwise speak French with perfect accents.

Like any complicated ritual act, speaking a language can be used to separate the ins from the outs. There are many ways to do this. You can freeze out those who don't know the language at all, those who speak it incorrectly, those who have the wrong accent.

Language facilitates the development of brains, thus enhances the separation of the more intelligent from the less. And the rich and powerful from the poor and the weak, because the elegant language of established power requires wealth and leisure to learn.

The sharing of language leads to loyalty. For many centuries in Europe second sons of rich families and intelligent boys from poor ones were consecrated to God by being taught Latin. The discipline of Latin set them apart, united them, and helped fit them for the discipline of the Church.

The more I thought about it the more I realized that the invention of language was a great step forward as a technique for controlling human behavior. Language makes it easier to herd people together and to tell them what to do. Learning to talk provides training in following rules. In particular, language conditions you to follow arbitrary rules, illogical rules, nonfacilitative, obstructive, and non-functional rules. This softens you up for following orders without questioning their source, their authority, their logic, or their utility.

Anyone who has learned a language can be conscripted as a soldier or a slave!

Of course you can chain and beat your soldiers and slaves, but that is an inefficient, stupid form of human control.

Right!

Army recruits are purposely schooled in the discipline of following orders without thought. Modern workers in both factories and offices do mindless, assembly-line jobs. So like faith, good morale, and patriotism, grammaticality—correct language use—requires unquestioning, thoughtless loyalty to a language.

I'll bet I was having so much trouble learning to speak French because I did not want to pledge allegiance to a foreign language.

René Descartes told a story that he had heard about apes. It was said that they are really people, but they do not talk for fear we would find out and put them to work.

You cannot get a thing to do something by talking to it unless it responds to language. Some people have not yet learned that it does no good to talk to rocks, plants, most animals, many Frenchmen, and God.

Locke thought human nature was completely malleable through application of the carrot and the stick. He thought this meant that human beings were infinitely perfectible. But others have seen this view as a threat to human freedom, for it suggests that we can become accustomed to and tolerant of any degree of oppression. An alternative view is Descartes's notion that there is an inviolable core of human dignity. Noam Chomsky interprets this to mean that all human beings are born with the ability to develop creative language use. Thus, generation of free thought can never be subdued. But if the generative rules of language are ever mapped in detail, I fear that this knowledge of the language machine will lead to even greater control of human beings.

To be independent is to be beyond rules and thus outside control. But for this you would have to be a Nietzschean superman possessing a private language with rules known to yourself alone. The true individual shares a language with no one, because anyone who knows your language—or even your name—has power over you.

This means that Wittgenstein's argument that private language is impossible, and that all language is necessarily communal, that you can have a language only as a member of a group of mutual language users, strikes against individualism. Descartes's claim that each human being is born with an inviolable sense of dignity, Locke's claim that each of us is born as a blank tablet on which any story at all can be written by experience, Nietzsche's claim that each of us can be an individual independent of every other, Chomsky's claim that human beings freely generate language, and Wittgenstein's claim that a single individual could not have a language and thus could not be human, for to be human is to be a member of a language-using group—all these positions have ideological implications and are political. Correct communal language use provides a paradigm for all those who desire to control others, and for all those who desire to be reined in, who want a leader or a master or a faith. Those who seek self-mastery and self-control are like Humpty-Dumpty, who insisted against great odds that he could use words to mean just what he pleased. "The question is," he said, "which is to be Master—that's all." And for whatever the king promised about sending horses and men, we know what happened to him.

It was a depressing prospect. To learn French I might have to give up my lifelong adherence to the doctrine of extreme individualism. I had been attracted by French radicalism only to discover that in language the French are hidebound conservatives.

I had gone deep and the prospect was bleak. But there was no possibility after I started Intensive French at the Alliance Française, four hours a day, five days a week, that I would quit before I finished the course.

The final exam at the end of Part IV was a dividing point. If you passed at the end of these four months, you could go on to the final two parts of what I now realized was a six-month course. And if not, not. I had scratched through the exams at the ends of Parts II and III, and I was full of hope—if not optimistic—about the final exam. It was to be given in four parts: oral, grammar, composition, and dictation.

The oral examination was given ten class days before the end of the course. We went, in groups of three, to the main building where a teacher who did not know us conducted the exam. The first part consisted of the three of us carrying on a discussion in a "situation" set by the teacher. We were supposed to be waiting in an airport for a plane whose takeoff was delayed for unspecified reasons. The other two— a Swedish girl and an Italian girl—were supposed to be frightened, and I was the calm old man. That didn't go so well. Then the examiner asked each of us why we wanted to learn French, and since we had already gone through that routine at the beginning of each month of class, on that we could talk.

I told the examiner how embarrassed I was to be a Cartesian scholar who could not speak French, and how I had set as a goal in life learning to speak well enough to hold my own in a circle of French Cartesian scholars. In the course of the discussion, the other two replied in response to the examiner's comment that it must be interesting to have a philosophy professor in the class, that it was, that I had given a very interesting lecture on the metaphysical foundation of depression. I had concluded ironically that Platonists who were in agony about not being able to reach perfection should convert therapeutically to Christianity because while there is no pity in Plato, Christ offers absolution.

"Did you understand my lecture?" I quickly asked the girls.

"Oh yes," they said, "you were very clear."

When we left, the examiner said, "Très bon" ("Very good"). I thought that meant we had passed. Now it seemed to me that I had a chance of passing the course, so over the weekend I studied continually. (I would have anyway.) Claude gave me dictations Saturday and Sunday. I was pretty sure I could pass the grammar exam, and maybe I could scratch through composition and dictation.

On Monday, I was ready for the grammar exam. I was a whiz on the subjunctive and conditional, but most of what I knew was unnecessary, for the exam was extremely easy. I missed "pas du _____" because I knew that "pas" was always followed by "de" and could not imagine what "pas du" could be. This is a good example of how one can read for sense and not for spelling, or how the words look, for the phrase is "pas du *tout*" ("not at all"), which I have surely read and understood and used thousands of times.

The next day the teacher went over similar material— but not the exam itself. I was sure that I had gotten almost everything right, and that I had passed the grammar exam. Composition and dictation were still to come. I continued studying.

I stayed in Paris—at first alone and then with Pat—in Michel Siffre's pied-à-terre apartment. It consisted of one small room with a large window out onto a busy, one-way street in one direction, and another small room with a large window out onto another busy, one-way street in the other direction. The refrigerator was in a third room, a storeroom that you had to go out into the hall and unlock a door to reach. The apartment was on the fourth floor, higher than the building across the street to the southwest, so there was a good view of clouds and sunsets and the night sky. It was in an old building in the Montparnasse part of Paris, postcard scenic, and very cozy. Years ago Michel had given Pat and me a set of keys to this apartment, and refused to take rent.

Paris is one of the most beautiful cities in the world, and one of the most congenial in which to live. This is because there are about a hundred square miles of streets with buildings rarely higher than eight floors (six stories, but in the European way of reckoning, this does not count the ground floor and the attic). The streets are sometimes wide, but even when they are narrow the buildings are low enough that you do not feel closed in. You are always aware of clouds and the blue sky during the day, and at night the moon and even bright stars hang right over the roof. One of the reasons Paris was so appealing to the Lost Generation of American writers in the 1920s is that this openness to the sky reminded them—so many from the Midwest—of home.

Americans have always loved Paris, but they have never found it easy to enter French life. American expatriates of the 1920s got to know some French communists, a Protestant writer, some lesbians, but not many nonmarginal establishment figures. It was not because the Americans could not speak French. Thirty years earlier, Henry James—who spoke French well—lived a year in Paris, and wanted to settle there, but he moved on to London because he said he knew he would never be accepted in Paris.

What makes Paris a city for people and for living is that the ground-floor level of almost all these buildings consists of small shops, while the seven floors above are apartments. Within a block of our apartment there were three bakeries, two butchers, three delicatessens, four small groceries, three restaurants, a pharmacy, a shoe-repair shop, two news-tobacco shops, three small hotels, a plumber, an upholsterer, a key maker, a cabinet maker, and many, many more. Tuesday and Friday mornings there was a large farmers' market a block away. On Sunday there was a wonderful flea market where Claude bought ancient postcards of caves for his collection. Two blocks away to the east and to the south were major streets with shops carrying all the goods Paris had to offer—clothes, furs, perfume, wine, cheese, furniture, and a thousand other things. Close by was a shop where wooden jigsaw puzzles were made and sold. Those that were more than toys retailed from three hundred dollars to over a thousand, and if you lost pieces, they would replace them. Another shop made and sold only bouquets of dried flowers. There were bookshops everywhere.

The streets are full of people late into the night. Neighbors know one another. One night we were eating in a restaurant and noticed that everyone stayed talking from table to table after they finished eating. About 11:00 the chef came out of the kitchen and was greeted by all. He sat down and noticed us immediately. He yelled to ask if we were of the neighborhood. Then he told us scandalous stories about people at the other tables, to great laughter all around. Don't ask for consistency. The French are as mean as can be. But when they go out to dinner they sit down at 8:30 or 9:00 and don't expect to get up until midnight. They have a good time. Even a foreigner can be of the neighborhood, and after a while you begin to feel that no place else is more like home.

It is safer in Paris than in many other major cities such as Rome or New York simply because the streets are for people. But watch out in the Metro.


I felt him bump my pocket, but did not react for a moment. Then I reached down frantically, and found my passport case was gone. It was a very existential feeling, appropriate for Paris, right out of Jean-Paul Sartre. I felt the absence of my passport case as though that absence were a solid thing.

The warning buzzer had sounded, the doors of the car were about to close. It was the morning rush at one of the most crowded Metro stations in Paris. People had been pouring in and out of the car. I grabbed the doors, held them open until I could get through and out onto the platform. There were hundreds of people rushing up the stairs. Three or four of them were running. I picked one out and ran after him. Of course I caught him, scaring him half to death, but he was not the thief. I suppose it was as well he wasn't. I might have been knifed.

I went up onto the street to the nearest police station. In the case had been my passport, driver's license, American Express card, Alliance Française ID, Bibliothèque Nationale ID, Washington University ID, and various other cards. There was also a 500 franc note, worth about $100. The police said not to worry about it, I would probably get my papers back. I went home and called to cancel the American Express card. Then I called the American consulate. They said to wait at least a week before applying for a new passport. I might get the old one back.

I had to study, so couldn't fret, but what a stupid thing to do! I had done everything wrong. First, there was no need to carry all those things. Second, I should not have carried my passport case in my pocket. Frenchmen may look silly carrying purses, or holding their billfolds in their hands, but they do know where they are. So, third, I should not have taken my hand off my pocket if that was where I was going to carry my passport case.

The next day in class the door opened and a woman asked if Richard Watson was in this class.

"Your papers are at the post office," she said, and gave me the address of a post office near the Metro stop where my pocket had been picked.

When the class was over, I took the Metro to the post office. I went to a window and said I had some papers there. The clerk was French and so instantly denied it. But another clerk looked up and beckoned to me. He handed me my passport case. He looked at me with annoyance, but said nothing. I suppose he recognized me from the many identity photographs in the case.

I opened the case and looked through it quickly. Everything had been gone through. Everything was still there. Except the 500 franc note.

I had done one thing right. That 500 franc note had not been hidden. It popped right out when the passport case was opened.

"They are professionals," The Professor explained to the class the next day. "When he opened the case and saw the 500 franc note, he thought that Ree-shar knew what he was doing. Five hundred francs is just about the right sum. So he was honor bound to put the passport case in a mailbox."

"If there had been no money," she said in answer to a question, "he would have dropped it in the sewer."

We had been warned many times to watch our belongings at the Alliance Française, which was said to be a regular mine for foreign passports. I had already had conciliatory fantasies that perhaps my identity would give some illegal immigrant a new life. But the Metro pickpockets are specialists. They take only money. They are very civilized.

I have remarked that Michel Siffre, my French landlord who refused to take rent, is the preeminent speleologist in France—a country where such exotica as bicycle racing and cave exploring are cared for as passionately as are baseball and football in America. Michel is also the best-known cave scientist in the world because for more than twenty-five years he has been conducting experiments in which he isolates people in caves, away from normal time clues, to study their bodily rhythms. The rhythms drift and lengthen, and some subjects have settled into forty-eight-hour "days" in which they sleep twelve hours and are fully awake, working, for thirty-six. Michel himself has stayed in a cave as a subject in isolation for six months.

Whenever I reoccupy Michel's apartment in Paris, it takes me several days to settle down. Another French caver, Francis Le Guen, once said of Michel's way of life that Michel does not live anywhere, he camps. But Francis did not quite get the Flaubertian *mot juste* for Michel's dwelling places. They are not camps, they are nests. Pack rat nests. Michel never throws anything away.

So when I entered his apartment in late May, although I had straightened it up the previous summer, and although I had been told that he had occupied it for only one week in the interim, I was not surprised to find it knee-deep in debris. Not only does Michel keep all newspapers, magazines, junk mail, and gum wrappers, he goes out of his way to collect giveaway descriptive literature—half a dozen duplicate copies of everything.

My rule is that I throw away nothing that he has collected. Perhaps I throw away a gum wrapper or two, but who is to know what use he might have for them? This restriction is difficult for me because I want to clean up, throw things out, and get on with it. After my father died, I threw away the check stubs he had kept all his life. Boy, was that a dumb thing to do.

Michel leaves newspapers folded open to articles that interest him. I gathered them all up, opened them out to full size, and made three stacks in the storeroom each three feet high. I shelved magazines in the storeroom, where there are two or three thousand now in rows, many of them folded open to an article that interested Michel. I sorted out and shelved his books. I did nothing with hundreds of sixteen millimeter films in large cans that were already stacked in the storeroom. Michel makes movies for television.

His personal papers and memorabilia at first defied ordering, but eventually I saw that old bills, tickets, envelopes, notes, fliers, letters, and the like fell together roughly in chronological order. They were the archaeological records of Michel's days, and once I saw that, I stacked them away more or less in order in filing boxes—for it was not that he didn't also have walls of bookshelves and filing boxes of all sorts, he just never used them systematically.

Michel apparently actually had been camping sometime during the past year, for on the living room floor were dumped an unfolded tent, a sleeping bag, and various other pieces of equipment. His clothes—I put them in the closet. Spoons and forks, cups and plates, pots and pans—on shelves in the entryway separating the two main rooms, where a hot plate sat on a trolley. After a week or so of picking up, categorizing, and shelving, I had room to lay out my own work and to shelve my own books. At a used furniture store down the street I bought an easy chair, a floor lamp, and some comfortable wooden kitchen chairs to replace some unsittable period-piece atrocities someone had given Michel. Finally, I could settle down to work.

Wasn't it a bit presumptuous of me to go through all of Michel's things? Didn't I even feel guilty about it? You can bet your buttons I did.

"You have destroyed the poetry of Michel's life," Jacques Chabert said to me.

I had done this thing to Michel's apartment the first time years ago, compulsively making it neater and neater, worrying continually what he would think and say, because it seemed to me that exactly what I was doing was messing with Michel's mind. But in that small apartment, I couldn't help myself, because when I work, I like to have all I need and only what I need carefully ordered before me. Anything extraneous distracts me, and what I don't need I get rid of. In my study in St. Louis, books and papers are neatly organized and filed according to projects. Everything is separated. Sometimes I go over it all ordering and discarding, and when I know exactly what is there, everywhere, I also know what I think, and then I can settle down, my mind is calm and relieved and full, and I can get to work.

Michel obviously worked and thought in a world entirely different from my own. Everything of his was interlaced and overlapped. Immersed in a jumble of all his things, he wrote his books, planned his experiments, his films, and his expeditions, and lived his life. It was the difference between a mystic and a rationalist, between a muddy-minded holist and a clear-minded analyst, I thought meanly as I turned into my mother and set about ruthlessly cleaning house. All those newsmagazine stories on this and that, for example. Michel, I snapped to myself, thinks they are worth something, but they're just journalism. If I wanted to know anything about those subjects, I'd go to the professional reports. He thinks there are buried treasures in this trash, but pull it apart to see what is really there, and it is gum wrappers. What I am destroying is Michel's bed of illusions, I thought grimly and self-righteously to myself.

It made me uneasy. Also, I wasn't being fair. Had I not, after all, shelved rows of photocopies and reprints of articles from professional journals, as well as the newsmagazines? And didn't Michel, after all, work in the media? And without being mystical or murky at all, wasn't it true that any collection of items, no matter how haphazard their interrelations, amounts to something far more than the mere itemization of its parts? I had myself discerned a chronological order in what first appeared to be mere wastepaper. Would Michel be furious and would I lose him as a friend? Not to mention the apartment?

Claude shook his head and "tched" his tongue at what I had done. Not that he wasn't sympathetic. Claude himself was a classic French rationalist, as far removed beyond my feeble essays at order as I was beyond Michel. The order of Claude's study—two floors up, in two rooms just like Michel's—put my own systems to shame. All of Claude's books on caves were cataloged and neatly arranged by multiple categories behind drawn curtains. Stamps, wine labels, comic strip panels, advertisements—anything on paper having a cave motif—were arranged in large folio-sized folders, mounted artistically—I mean with lots of blank space around them to set them off—on light cardboard sheets. Thousands of cave postcards were categorized and filed. Cave maps in progress were here, manuscripts being written were there, manuscripts being edited there, the proofs of the next issue of *Grottes et Gouffres,* which Claude edits, there. File cabinets held reprints and correspondence. There were his worldwide affairs as president of the International Speleological Union's Commission on the World's Longest and Deepest Caves, his bibliographies of books read with detailed notes on cards about each, his bibliography of cave books, printed copies of his bibliography of the works of the father of modern speleology, E.-A. Martel, his present work in progress, a bibliography of everything written in all languages on Turkish caves, on which he had advanced in the first typing to items by authors whose name began with the letter C, of which there were some three hundred entries. In the closet were his collections of complete works of French literature and philosophy, rows of literary magazines all beginning with volume 1, number 1, and folders of pictures and prints of caves. In the front room were several hundred copies of his book on the long and deep caves of the world, and the mantel of the fireplace was stacked high with books waiting to be read. True French rationalism is awesome when encountered in two small rooms.

"Michel's mother actually is," Claude confided to me, "Italian."

My worries, as usual, were ridiculous. Two months after I had settled in, I heard panting, something being dragged up the stairs, a muffled "Merde," the sound of struggling with keys, and then Michel opened the door. There he stood, a small man with a bullet-shaped head set on solid, sloping shoulders over a thick chest. He was puffing and grinning from ear to ear.

"Magnificent!" he said, looking around. "A palace! And so light!"

I had also washed scum off the windowpanes, letting in one-third more sun than formerly.

Michel shrugged off a backpack, then dragged a large duffel bag into the apartment.

"No, no, no, I can do it myself," he protested as we went down the stairs and up again, twice. There were four more enormous duffel bags. We dragged them up the four flights of stairs.

Michel collapsed on the couch, his tie askew, his white shirt drenched with sweat.

"Don't rush like that, Michel," I said. "We're not getting any younger. You'll kill yourself."

He nodded, grimaced, took off his suit jacket and tie and tossed them down.

"It is necessary," he said, looking at my Levi's, "to dress with some dignity at our age and in our positions."

He—like my mother—did not think well of my wardrobe, of the careless attire of American college professors. We could teach in such clothes back home, but if we wanted to be taken seriously in France, we should wear suits and ties.

What I had forgotten in my needless worries about what Michel would think is that he always carries with him a traveling nest. When he got his breath, he began to take newspapers, magazines, books, papers, folders and files, photographs, films, pens, pencils, rulers, scissors, tape, a sleeping bag . . . clothes . . . and stack them around him until he was at home. In a twinkling, the apartment looked much as it had before I moved in. Michel was ready to go to work.

Several days later I came back from class to find Michel pensively reading his way along the shelves I had ordered, pulling this and that out to add to his stacks of paper.

"This is wonderful," he said absently. "I had no idea what I had here. I can use some of these things."

A week later he left again for Nice. His old four-liter Citroen, without papers, without insurance, not by plan but as the result of unbelievably intricate complications, was stuffed with a ton of books and papers and clothes from the apartment and storeroom. I forgot to mention that Michel's apartment contained over four thousand copies of his book *Les Animaux des Gouffres et des Cavernes.* The publisher had given them to him when the book was discontinued. It was a large, heavy book. The bed in the apartment was a mattress on a platform of these books, the couch was another mattress on such a platform, the bookshelves were boards supported by stacks of these books, as was the desk and the work table. Michel took two hundred copies with him to Nice. It was a drop in the bucket.

After he had gone, I picked up again. He had left as much as he had taken along. I ordered it, shelved it, and went back to my monastic student's life.

The French have a doomlike sense of the finality, of the irrevocable and intractable nature, of human acts. You count your money carefully and think seriously before you buy a sheet of stamps at a French post office, for if you suddenly remember that you need some money to buy bread and try to hand half the sheet back, the postal clerk simply shakes his or her head. Never fill out forms in any French office unless you are fully committed, for the moment you hand them over they become official documents, thereafter not only out of your hands to take back or to alter, but also out of the hands of the person to whom you gave them. And of course it is hopeless to run to move your car when you see a policewoman writing a ticket, because nothing can be altered from the instant she sets pencil to paper. Very seldom can you recoup, although I once did. In a bakery where I bought a raisin roll every morning, I carelessly accepted in change a ten franc note with a large piece of one corner torn off. The woman shrugged when I pointed this out to her. All that day I tried to pass that ten franc note, but no shopkeeper would accept it. The next morning I went to the bakery as usual and bought my raisin roll. I reached over and picked it up and took a bite out of it as I slid the torn ten franc note across the counter. The woman glared at me. I showed her the raisin roll, with one corner bitten off. I shrugged my shoulders. She counted out my change.

You can't learn unless you make mistakes. When I first went to France I had not yet learned to like wine, so I suspected that all the hullabaloo about French cuisine was the result of people drinking so much with their meals that they didn't notice how bad the food was. Later, at better restaurants, I began to like some of the French wines. Then, whether because of the conflict of interests initiated when my parents' genes were fused to make me, or because of

my Grandma Penwell's Methodist diatribes about the de-
mon rum, physiologically or psychologically, my stomach
rebelled. After drinking wine for dinner, about 2:00 A.M. I
would wake up with violent stomach cramps, vomiting, and
diarrhea. After about the fourth time this happened, Pat
said, "You don't learn from experience, do you?" I no longer
drink wine.

I made a list of things you can get wrong in a dictation:

1. The word itself.
2. Mistaking a phrase for a word.
3. Mistaking a word for a phrase.
4. Spelling.
5. Number.
6. Gender.
7. Tense.
8. Conjugation.
9. Not contracting when you should because contractions
   are not arbitrary but are necessary in French.
10. Contracting when you should not.
11. Accent marks left off.
12. Accent marks wrongly added.
13. Punctuation (a very large number of possibilities here,
    of course).
14. Gaps when you write so fast that you leave words out.
15. Putting in extra words.

There are certainly more. During dictations, I made many
of these mistakes as I wrote frantically to keep up. When I
had time to go over my text afterward to think about it, I
could correct many of my errors. But we were given only

two or three minutes to check our work, and this was not time enough.

I understood most of the words in the dictations. But it was becoming clear to me that the chances were slim of my making few enough errors to pass the dictation exam. Even if I had time to correct all the stupid mistakes, there were details of accents and spellings and gender that I simply did not know. They did not affect my comprehension of spoken French, but they counted against me.

This matter of understanding continued to be highly relative. When people spoke to me directly and I knew what we were talking about—French grammar, Cartesian philosophy, cave exploring, food, comparison of things French with things American—I could understand quite well. But trying to comprehend people talking on the street or on the radio was often like tuning in on an unknown tongue. Most frustrating was to be talking quite well with Claude and Nicky, and then have them turn to address a couple of sentences to each other that were completely unintelligible to me.

I did progress. Thanks to Maya's six months of drilling, my Alliance Française teachers said my accent was passable. I could speak to French people who understood and replied with no hesitation, as though they did not even consider the possibility that I might not understand. This was an advance of many orders of magnitude over my early days at the Bibliothèque Nationale. It also meant that people talked to me so rapidly or colloquially that I sometimes did not catch it all.

Frenchwomen speak more precisely and articulate better than do Frenchmen, who have a tendency to mumble. I was sorry that all my Alliance Française teachers were women, for I needed practice listening to men. I did talk a lot to Claude, who usually, shall we say, moved over the landscape of his language with less attention to its ups and downs than would communicate a full sense of its contours. A more serious problem with Claude was that he understood English well, and thus could decipher strings of French words in English sentence forms that the ordinary Frenchman could not.

Once the young students recovered from their astonishment at seeing an old professor in their classes, they rallied behind me. They encouraged me in my slow progress. They were, as my mother might have been had I been doing a little better, proud of me. Their support reminded me of some years previously when Pat and I were jogging through a forest in the Cévennes, a most beautiful part of France. We came upon a French couple who were somewhat younger than us. They had packsacks, boots, and staffs, and gaped as we came breezing along and passed them. We already knew that joggers were rare in this part of France. Little children would run out to identify us. "Footing!" they would shout, which is what it is called on French television. We got past the hikers, and then the man found his voice and shouted after us with great, heartfelt enthusiasm, "Courage!"

That first month of classes at the Alliance Française was relaxed and easygoing. Claire covered the material well, but often did not seem to take the class very seriously. This was understandable given that students were always dropping in and out. But when Claire suggested that on the last day of class we go to a museum, I was glad that several students protested. The course was not cheap, and I have already mentioned that paying your tuition to the Alliance Française was one of those acts that cannot be revoked. Claire compromised by saying that we would go after the break.

The parting on the last day reminded me of when I was sixteen years old. During the summer of 1947, I was a trail guide for burro pack trips at Philmont Scout Ranch in New Mexico. I guided six groups of Boy Scouts on ten-day trips through the mountains. Each group of ten to twenty was made up of boys from all over the United States, and at the end of the trip we had gotten to know each other well. Parting was accompanied with vows of eternal friendship. In a trunk in the attic I have all their names and addresses, and postcards from one or two. I never saw even one of them again.

I noticed a change immediately at the beginning of Part III, my second month of classes. We had passed exams to advance to the second half of the four-month course, and my new classmates were older, had understandable accents (some in the earlier class were terrible), and knew the grammar. For the first time I was with students who had studied a considerable amount of French before coming to the Alliance Française. Numbers of them were taking the course for college credit. There were even a few—the Syrian, the

Romanian—who spoke French fluently, but needed the language certificate.

I knew the grammar when I read it, but it was not there when I tried to write or speak. So I read carefully through the wonderful Bescherelle grammar book. I studied the superb Bescherelle verb book, particularly the seventy-seven pages outlining the seventy-seven different conjugations of French verbs. Perhaps I should also have studied the third Bescherelle volume on orthography, which consists solely of lists of differently spelled words that sound alike. But there were thousands of them, and I knew they would just merge together if I tried.

After Claude had given me a few dictations, starting with one from Balzac that was totally beyond me, he asked me to give some English dictations to him.

"We don't have dictations in English," I protested.

He didn't believe me and, in any case, insisted. So I made some up.

> Saul was quite a sight when he threw down from the peak the guild's gilded awl right where he stood on the site where people wait to cite, or write their orders for certain weights of peeled peas unless they're impeded in their aims by piqued pianists throwing orange peels out the doors of their dormitories with peals of laughter.

Claude did remarkably well on his English dictations and was very proud of himself. I argued that there was nothing quite so tricky in English as the sound in French that can be spelled "se," "ce," "ces," "c'est," "s'e," and probably a dozen other ways.

After Pat arrived, Michel came again for a week in Paris. This time he made most of his nest in Claude's study upstairs, but he did keep some of his things in what was, we protested, after all, his very own apartment. One rainy day, he started to go out and Pat said, "Michel, aren't you going to wear your raincoat?"

"I left it on the train," Michel said with a very sad look on his face. "It was brand new, and I left it on the train."

"But Michel," Pat said, "when you arrived, I hung it in the closet with your other clothes."

"What clothes?" Michel asked. He rushed to the closet and opened the door to look, then came back into the living room pulling on his raincoat. Beaming, he said, "I would *never* have thought to look for it there. I was sure I had left it on the train."

I have always thought my bad spelling was due to inattention as to whether words end, say, with "an" or "on," and the like. Would not impatient inattention also explain how I can look up the spelling of a word, clamp the dictionary shut, and then turn to my writing and still not know how to spell it? I had gone through the procedure of looking it up; did I have to remember it, too? And doesn't everyone now and then reverse letters and numbers—"57" for "75" and even "Nood Gight"? Just today I asked for the "palt and sepper" at lunch, and as long as I can remember I have made that kind of exchange of initial letters perhaps once a week. Is that a kind of dyslexia? It really is not a serious problem in speaking and spelling. What is serious is my inability to listen to sounds and repeat them back. I was poor at memorizing poems and piano pieces in my youth. Again, this was attributed by both my teachers and me to a combination of laziness and impatience, to that same refusal to spend boring hours practicing that drove me from the chemistry lab when I was a freshman in college.

But now I was trying. I was practicing. I was listening and repeating back. I read Georges Simenon's mystery novels out loud in French, trying to accumulate an auditory vocabulary. But time and again when I wanted to use a French word that I knew I knew, a word I would recognize instantly if I either read it or heard it, it would not come up. I could not hear nor see it in my mind.

"You must," said The Professor, of all people, "all go dance in the streets on Bastille Day."

It was a four-day holiday. The Alliance Française had as many holidays as the Turks, and that's a lot. And each day of classes missed increased how much you were paying for each of the others, and decreased my chances of passing the final exam. Catch me dancing in the streets! I sat home and went over all my notes, ordering and rewriting them. I *did* know this stuff. Why, then, was I still so low in my class? Why did I make stupid, simple errors, one after the other? How much practice did it take, not to be perfect, but to pass?

As I sat working at Michel's desk, or staring moodily out the window while I listened to the radio for the painful half hour that was minimally prescribed by The Professor,

I would often hear the noise of another triumph of French engineering—the bottle truck.

Throughout Paris there are large green steel containers five feet tall and just as fat on street corners for the deposit of empty bottles. The signs on the containers say that unbroken bottles will be reused and broken glass recycled. Citizens are thanked for their cooperation.

Deposition proceeds at all hours, and one of the typical dead-of-night sounds you wake up to in Paris is the steady chink-chink-chink of a case of empty wine bottles being thrust one by one through bottle-sized holes into one of these steel containers by a conscientious citizen.

An enormous green truck labors through the streets to collect the bottles. The truck stops by one of the large containers, and . . . It took me months to find out what happened next. The truck arrived twice a week at the container at the end of the block where the two one-way streets met. (The apartment building was wedge shaped.) Determined as I was to see how it was done (because I couldn't imagine, there being no doors visible in the steel containers, only four round holes for bottles), I was always too late. I would hear a tremendous crash of bottles. "Damn!" I would say, and rush to the front room window, out of which I could just see the snout of the green truck down beyond the end of the building, and then to the bedroom window, out of which the back of the truck was just visible, while the building in between blocked my view of the crucial maneuver. If I ran down four flights of stairs and to the end of the street, the green truck would be just disappearing around a corner. Knowing that it came at approximately 11:00 A.M. on Tuesdays and Fridays, I staked it out by taking my work down and waiting, but when I did the truck did not show, and I had to leave at noon for my 12:30 class. When I forgot to stake it out, it always came on time.

Then one day on my way home from class at 5:00, I came upon the truck and stood amazed, witnessing the entire spectacle.

The truck stops by one of the large containers. A great hinged and angled arm set on the roof of the truck cab gropes over and lowers a round steel plate about two feet in diameter onto the flat top of the container. Spring-spiraled electric wires run from the plate to the cab of the truck. The truck driver hooks two chains to loops on the top of the container, but they are mere safety devices, for the steel plate is in fact a magnet, through which electricity courses when the truck engine is raced.

The arm strains, the magnet grips, and it lifts the heavy container of bottles, swings it ponderously over the truck bed, and thumps it down, sometimes three or four times, until a large projecting trigger on the container's bottom is released. Then the arm jerks up triumphantly, raising the steel container rapidly as its bottom flops down. Bottles and broken glass rush out onto the steel bed of the truck or onto other glass. There is a most wonderfully satisfying crash and smash of a magnitude of which small boys (prior to the invention of the bottle truck) could only dream. Then the container is swung back over its base, the truck driver latches up its bottom, and the container is seated, ready to collect more bottles in the night.

The French love nothing more than the good solid clang of heavy steel on heavy steel. Thirty years ago when I first came to Paris, I was pleased with large, ugly, square, metal vending machines on building walls. Through the dim glass front you could see rows of small cardboard boxes stacked up inside. In each box was a trick, a toy, a trinket, new, mysterious, and until the box was open, unknown. Put a franc in the slot, pull a knob, there was a terrific smash and bang as though miraculously a large man inside that small box had hit a heavy lever with a sledgehammer, and one of the boxes thumped down into the tray below. These vending machines are still there, working. I am a sentimental fool, and tears come to my eyes at the devotion to tradition they exhibit. Those machines are still on the walls of buildings at such a height that only an adult can put a franc in the slot. An interested six-year-old could never reach that high. Think now of generations of indulgent young French mamas and papas, dropping a franc in the slot, pulling the knob, and with a resounding metallic bang, buying joy for a waiting child.

On Midsummer Night's Eve, I walked for hours from well above the old Opéra on the Right Bank to Michel's apartment far past the Luxembourg Gardens on the Left Bank. There were people everywhere, and street entertainers—I passed mimes, storytellers, street theater, musicians, everything from music hall whistlers to string quartets. It remained light until nearly midnight.

I stopped to watch the game the kids play three stories above the street on the flat marble roof of the Lafayette shops below the Montparnasse Tower, the only skyscraper in Paris. This stretch of marble is a hundred and fifty yards long and fifty yards wide. The kids are on roller skates.

They begin with one standing in the center waiting. Then a dozen or twenty or more skaters start from one end and skate toward him. Those he tags must join him and try to tag the others on the next sweep.

I love the timing. The skaters reach the other end, stand bent over with their hands on their knees, puffing. Then they begin to line up and, without a signal, one of them starts skating gracefully down the length toward the center, in a curving trajectory to gain speed, while the others string out behind him until a whole phalanx of skaters is bearing down at top speed on the one or two or three taggers waiting. A wild and fast game.

Who owns the roof? Would the game be permitted in New York? St. Louis?

Parents rent small sailboats for their children to sail in the big round basin in Luxembourg Gardens, and this tradition certainly goes back at least to the seventeenth century. "Vite! Vite!" ("Quick! Quick!") a very small little girl kept yelling at her mother, as she ran around the edge of the basin, trailing her boat stick twice as long as she was. She was very good at leaning over to turn her boat around to point out into the basin by putting the end of the stick on the deck projection and shoving. Much more skill than you would expect anyone that size to have. I had a pang of nostalgia for my own daughter, not for the sophisticated, French-speaking twenty-five-year-old, but for the little girl she once was, racing through Luxembourg Gardens to be lifted up for the first pony ride ever, a look of wild excitement on her face strong enough to illuminate the whole wide world.

The statue with the upraised arm had a pigeon sitting on its fist and another on its head—the park pigeons take turns to keep it always occupied for photographers, and take their pay in bread crumbs.

As I got on toward the apartment in the Fourteenth Arondissement, there was a dog playing the game with his stiff old master as tagger. The dog ran toward his master and veered away just enough not to get caught and have his leash snapped on. I pointed my finger at the dog, and, watching me, he let himself be caught on the next rush. Master and dog looked at me as the leash was attached, and at least the old man smiled.

Long after midnight, nearing home, I stopped in front of the local café. Standing in a row, thirty men, women, and children, each with some kind of percussion instrument, were making music. It rose and fell like the sound of cicadas in the trees. Two young men in band uniforms, carrying large snare drums, returning from some parade, came by and joined in. It was a joyful noise, out of the depths of the human psyche, when all the world was young.

Old Paris, it lifts your heart. Also, alas, the top of your head. The noise is insupportable, the ubiquitous din. Those streets are canyons down which continuously roar automobiles, trucks, motorcycles, police cars and ambulances with sirens and klaxons shrieking and clanging at near the top of the range of human tolerance. There are no speed limits and everyone drives as fast as possible. Motorcycles and motor scooters and many trucks and buses are without mufflers. Trucks stop in narrow streets to make deliveries and dozens of cars pile up behind them, honking. The noise solidifies up and down the narrow streets. There is the noise of bulldozers and heavy construction everywhere.

But sometimes you wake up late at night. What is it? For a few moments there is silence. Then you hear a car race by, in the distance there is a rumble, the uproar begins again, and you drift back to sleep.

Before dawn the garbage trucks come by (every day, including Sunday). Garbage cans are attached to projections on the back of the truck, the engine races, the cans are lifted up and over and dumped with a resounding bang, and then clattered back down onto the street. Street-cleaning trucks go by, and always the buses. The shops open and close with the crash of heavy steel shutters and gates; every apartment window has shutters that are slammed shut at night and open in the morning. Television sets boom out of apartments, radios roar in the streets, the bistros are full of people shouting far into the night. Why do they shout? Kids laugh and babies scream. The sparrows twitter and the pigeons coo.

Over there on the Right Bank, the old Opéra sits at the top of one of the most magnificent boulevards in the world, along which are some of the grandest shops. And you sit there at a famous sidewalk café at the main crossroads for every tourist in the Western World. You smile at your companion, hold hands, drink an aperitif. You don't talk. The roar of cars and trucks and buses in the street is so deafening that you can hardly think, but the shattered thought drifts through your head that someone had a good idea, but something went wrong. Paris is a beautiful city. It was made for people. But you can't live there for longer than a few months at a time, for after that you have to leave to escape the noise.

Whenever I spend any time in Paris, I swear that I will never return to stay there for more than a week. But I always do.

I wonder if, with a trillion dollars, one could put most Parisian traffic underground and develop a system of silent electric conveyances for necessary surface transport? And what would the result be? It is striking how many Parisian professors and intellectuals are killed by being hit by trucks and cars in the street. Think of the slaughter if vehicular traffic were silent.

Anyway, my daughter says Tokyo's where it's at now. Paris has had it.


Claude said it would take two years of residence for me to learn to speak French. But I had, off and on, lived in France longer than that already. The problem was that I was not very sociable. Pat and I once rented a nice isolated cottage outside a village where we sat and wrote. We went to the market twice a week for groceries. There wasn't time to natter with the natives. Even if they would have.

The Professor recommended that we go to the Luxembourg Gardens and find some old person sitting alone. "Go up to them and ask them to tell you their life story. That is a time-honored way in France to learn to speak French."

I don't know. I never heard of anyone who tried it, and I'd advise anyone who did to stand well back while asking. Some of those old people can spit a long way.

Well, who knows? Paris actually isn't what it used to be. Insidiously, progress is gnawing at the city. There are now supermarkets, and even frozen foods. In Paris! A few years ago big operators managed to change the law that booksellers could not go below publishers' list prices, so now there is an enormous cut-rate bookstore in Paris where all books are sold at a discount. (I refuse to give its name, but no one has any trouble finding out.) That bookstore now sells half the books purchased in Paris, which is devastating to the thousands of small bookshops for which Paris is famous.

The building height law has been successfully fought in many areas, so that high-rise office and apartment buildings are going up all over Paris. Wherever they appear, the shops at street level disappear, and the street becomes a desolate, windswept canyon, just like New York City. It will take a while, but eventually Paris will be modernized.

Of course, the TWA clerk would point out that had the French fought for their country during World War II, Hitler would have seen to it that Paris was destroyed, as were so many other European cities. Then it would be already modern, as are so many of the cities in Germany. Many of those Parisian buildings are very old. A German who worked in Paris and lived in Michel's apartment building was always complaining to me about the dirtiness of the buildings and all things French. "I hate these dirty Frenches," he said, in English.

De Gaulle was sensitive to this problem. He ordered the removal from the streets of Paris of what he took to be two very offensive items—prostitutes and pissotières. Prostitutes and pissotières were duly banished from the streets.

I will not describe a prostitute, but a pissotière is one of the great successes—I mean really—of French engineering. In Paris it is, or was, a sheet of steel fretwork about four feet wide elegantly curved into a large *S* and then set up on edge on posts on a street corner. Pissotières also had steel-capped roofs to keep off the rain. They were, of course, painted dark green. Inside each curve of the *S* was a urinal. You, that is, a man, could step inside and take a piss. Of course your legs stuck out below the sheet of steel, and your head above. But you could take on an abstracted look, whistle, and pretend that people walking by didn't know what you were doing. People walking by, except for American tourists, in fact paid absolutely no attention to what you were doing.

The result of removing prostitutes and pissotières from the streets is as follows. Whereas a man knows perfectly well where to go in Paris today to find a prostitute, he often can find nowhere to piss. There are those new pay toilets that scrub themselves after each use (another marvel of French engineering), but they are few and far between. Thus, all Frenchmen being as casual about pissing as male dogs, some will turn on the sidewalks in Paris and piss against the building walls. One thus has to watch out not only for dog shit on the sidewalks, but also for puddles of piss. I don't know whether Paris always smells faintly of urine because of this, or because the famous sewers are not sealed off adequately under the streets.

Turning now to calls of nature that visit women, it was difficult for women even in the days of pissotières, the more so because it was easy for men. When our daughter was three years old and we were traveling one summer, Pat swore she was going to make a fortune by writing a guide titled *Where to Find a Toilet in Europe.* Besides the elusive new pay toilets, there *are* a few public toilets in Paris, but they keep bankers' hours. And try to find one on the huge park in front of the Eiffel Tower. There is one of the world's greatest street organs, but no public toilet. The park is visited by millions of tourists every year, some of whom do have to relieve themselves. You will confirm this fact for yourself with unpremeditated looks into the few bushes and hedges thereabouts, even though you did not actually have in mind checking to see. Cafés, bars, and restaurants are very difficult to crack because their proprietors keep close watch and turn back noncustomers. In desperation, you can rush into a hotel, up the stairs, and into a hall toilet, but this works only if you know where it is and are moving fast enough not to be stopped.

The toilets in train stations and museums are guarded by tough concierges who demand payment before letting you in. Not that you are unwilling to pay, but what if you don't have exact change? The first time our daughter ever went to a public toilet by herself was because of this. The summer she was three and a half, she and Pat were in Luxembourg Gardens, where there is one (count them, one) public toilet for one of the larger and more strolled central city parks in the Western World. Anna had to go, so Pat took her, but she had only fifty centimes in change, enough for one.

"No, madame," the concierge said firmly, holding Pat back. "Fifty centimes, one person."

She would not change a ten franc note. She would not let Pat go in. Triumphantly, Anna went alone.

One deplores the spread of American fast food restaurants in the major cities of Europe, but they do have one advantage. When a hundred people are pushing up to the counters in McDonald's, there is no way to tell whether you are a customer or not. The French closed down a public toilet on the most touristed street on the Left Bank, boulevard Saint Michel, but McDonald's opened a restaurant there that makes up for it. Even so, the proprietors are French. I was stopped at the top of the stairway down to the toilets in a Burger King in the usual French fashion. The proprietor thrusts his body and his raised eyebrows in your way and announces that his is not a public toilet.

But it was a Burger King! This was the last straw. I glared at him and said in a very loud voice, in French, "If you are going to insult French cuisine by running an American fast food joint in Paris, then it is necessary that you permit Americans to use the toilets," and I strode right at him. Furious, he stepped aside and let me go.

I should not leave the toilet scene in Paris without making two further comments. There are still many Turkish toilets in Paris, although those in the Bibliothèque Nationale have, to everyone's great relief, been replaced with regular stools.

It is almost impossible to read a book in a Turkish toilet. A Turkish toilet consists basically of a large piece of porcelain on the floor through which there is a hole and on which are two raised projections in the shape of reversed footprints on which you are to place your feet. People who have not used such a toilet all their lives can get into real trouble, and you are advised to plan carefully how you are going to rise back up again before you crouch down. They are flushed by pulling a chain hanging down the back wall. Take hold of the chain, but don't pull it yet. Step outside the cubicle, be ready to close the door, then pull the chain and jump back. Otherwise you might have to change your socks.

Second, this digression reminds me that we had right in Michel's apartment a candidate for winner in the game of French Engineering. On floor level at the back of the toilet stool, which otherwise was perfectly normal, was a large box. When you flushed the toilet, everything went into this box where an electric motor was automatically started and there was a loud grinding noise as what was flushed was ground thoroughly before being passed on into the French sewer system. I don't know why Michel had this attachment. None of the other toilets in the building had one, and I have never seen one anywhere else, except in the window of the plumber across the street who installed Michel's toilet. I believe at the time of installation Michel was either on an expedition in Guatemala or underground. The grinder is not for what you might think, because Michel had a handwritten note taped to the toilet warning you not to put sanitary napkins or anything else out of the ordinary down the toilet. But his most important notice was that you were under no circumstances ever to flush the toilet if the electricity was off, for otherwise it would back up and cover the floor with MERDE!!! Finally, you should not flush the toilet after 10:00 P.M. or before 8:00 A.M. Otherwise the neighbors would complain about the noise.

"When I grow up," I said in the general class go-around when our last teacher asked us near the end of the course to tell what we planned to do with the rest of our lives, "I want to be a speaker of French."

I asked, "Why are all the final exams given a week or more before the end of the course?"

"So we can correct them," the teacher said in surprise. "You want to know if you passed, don't you?"

I have tried to find a way to characterize the teacher of Part IV, my third month at the Alliance Française. I cannot remember her name or what she looked like. For a while, I thought of referring to her here as the lazy teacher, but that is not right. She did her work. She was more conventional than Claire and The Professor, and she assigned exercises out of our awful textbook, as they seldom did. She did not correct the exercises.

"The correct answers are in the back of the book," she said.

Any teacher knows that this is not adequate. You have to explain to students why the answers are correct and show each student individually where he or she went wrong.

Moreover, there were answers in the back of the book for only about half the exercises she assigned.

"They are so easy, that's why no answers are given," she said.

We were given the dictation and the composition exams on the same day. The dictation was very simple. The teacher even apologized for it. I understood every word, but that was the mere beginning. I checked my work over as systematically as a few minutes allowed, trying to concentrate as the others handed in their papers, and finally with the teacher standing over me saying that I really had to turn in my exam now, I was the last to give up the ghost.

The composition exam consisted of a paragraph in which a situation was developed. A man's sister had called him in the middle of the night. He had not seen her for years. She said he must come to her hotel room immediately and bring a large sum of money. She was in great distress. "Continue the story."

I had been warned about my compositions before, but I could not help myself.

> The man rapidly gathered up all the silverware and other valuables in his apartment and locked them in the wall safe. He put all his money there, too, except for 5,000 francs, which he sealed in an envelope and put in his pocket. Then he went to his sister's hotel room. She was hysterical. He gave her the envelope. She tore it open and threw the ten 500 franc notes on the floor. It wasn't enough money. No, she couldn't tell him what it was for. She would die if she didn't have more. She needed 500,000 francs. If he couldn't

get it all that night, then 50,000 francs now, and the rest tomorrow. She fell sobbing at his feet. After a while, her brother quietly got up and went out the door. As he left, she raised up and screamed after him, "You have killed me!" The door closed gently behind him.

She got up and went into the bathroom and washed her face. She picked up the 500 franc notes and put them in her purse. Then she went downstairs and across the street to the Casino, where she bought fifty 100 franc chips and then walked regally over to the roulette wheel.

Yes, yes, I *know*. But I did know how to write all that, rapidly, in French. I used only words and tenses that I was sure of. I knew it was too complicated, too involved. Better I should have used a story about Dick and Jane from my second grade reader. "See Dick run. Dick runs to Jane's hotel." Like that. But I didn't. I thought it was probably all right.

The next day the teacher gave us exercises to do in class while she sat correcting exams at her desk. No, they were not our exams, she said, everyone corrected exams from other classes. An American secondary school teacher said she thought it would be better if teachers corrected the exams of their own students, because they knew their work. Our teacher rolled her eyes to the ceiling and went back to her work. We would know how we had done at the end of the week.

I made the rounds, by phone, of the Parisian Cartesian scholars.

"I'm tied up now. Call me back in ten days. Or, better, give me your phone number. I'll give you a call in ten days."

None of them ever called me back, so why did I bother to call them back? What did I have in mind? I believe that I thought that was what I was supposed to do. I had published reviews of books by all of them. They knew my work. We had similar interests. We did constitute members of a special, rather small community, did we not? Shouldn't we get to know one another? Talk about our work? That sort of thing. Hmmm . . . ?

You might think so, but in fact a lot of that is sheer baloney. People in the sciences often have important new information to impart to one another and things to talk about, and often they even work together in teams, but this is seldom the case for humanist scholars. Even when they are working, say, on the same person or period, each is concerned with a special aspect of it. Even if two scholars are working on exactly the same subject using exactly the same materials, they will present different interpretations, and be in competition, not in collusion. There is no point in arguing face-to-face; they can insult each other adequately when they review each other's books.

If scholars do talk to one another, all they have to talk about is their own work. Few people can either challenge or help you in conversation, because they have not read exactly the things you have, so mostly you just tell them what you are working on. They tell you what they are working on. All of you say, "That's interesting," and get back to your own work. Oh, sometimes you learn something useful at conferences, but I exaggerate only slightly. The real point of getting together is to make contacts. The fact was, as a contact I was not wired into the Parisian power circuit, so why should any of them plug into me?

Nevertheless, I persisted. I must have, like Michel, been feeling the urge to nest. But as it became abundantly clear that I was not going to penetrate the Cartesian circle, something more motivated me. I simply wanted to know what, if I kept pestering them, they would do. I wanted response, interaction. Like the little boy with the stick with the horse's-head handle that he stuck into the ear of the lion that then ate him, I was with perverse excitement driven by curiosity to see what would happen if I took my stick and whacked the nest of Parisian Cartesian scholars, even though I knew it was filled with hornets.

I did, finally, one day, manage to make a luncheon engagement with a Cartesian scholar. Not Professor Marion, who was very busy but was going to get back to me. No, it was with Father Armogathe, whose work interested me just as much. He was in charge of one of the largest churches in Paris. That morning he had had a funeral, and he was late for our engagement because he had had at the last minute to visit a sick parishioner. Then he had to find a packet of manuscripts to send off by messenger to a publishing house where he was an editor. After that, he took me to a fine restaurant where we had a nice talk about things Cartesian. But he was also chaplain of a college and had to rush off to officiate there that afternoon. He talked a bit about the lecture he was preparing for the next day, because he was also a professor at the university. Besides the book he was editing and another he was writing, he was putting together a bibliography of the worldwide critical writings on Descartes. Although I had invited him to lunch, he refused to let me pay. I had not actually noticed the stings, but when we parted my face was red. I am slightly skeptical, but do you suppose all of them were so busy?

"I'm tied up now. Can you call back in ten days? Or, better, give me your phone number . . ."

After scoring with one Cartesian scholar, I did not get around to following up on any more of my calls.

A few days after the last of the four final exams at the Alliance Française, the door to our classroom opened, and a very severe looking woman carrying a large register entered. It was clear that she was important. Without preliminaries, she read off the names of the people who had passed the examination. As your name was read off, you were to go forward to get your card stamped. Then you could buy— for $12.50—a certificate, and you could advance to the final two months of the course, which I had very recently learned was in French Conversation. The first four months were the grammatical preliminaries to talking.

Of the twenty in my class who took the exams, four names were not called. They were those of the nice Austrian boy who never studied, two Greeks who did, and me. One of the Greeks went forward, questioned the woman angrily, then went back to get his bag and stalked out saying loudly that the Alliance Française was not a good school. The Austrian and the other Greek had not come to class since the last exam. My other classmates and I tried not to look at one another.

Then the teacher said to me, "Richard, aren't you going to get your card stamped?"

"I think I didn't pass," I replied.

I was grateful that she seemed surprised. She went quickly over to the important woman, looked at the register, and shook her head.

I took this opportunity to go up to the desk.

"Can I see my exams?" I asked

From being sympathetic, the teacher now became hard.

"No, not at all," she said.

"Can I see my grades?"

"No."

"But I would like to know what I did wrong."

"Not possible."

"How can I improve if I can't have an analysis of my exams?" I persisted.

She turned away in exasperation.

I was quite angry. At myself both for flunking the exams and for having thought that I might pass them even though I had earlier anticipated that I would not. It was also my first encounter with the French system of not even giving out grades, let alone analyses of examinations. But I, too, turned away.

It was the first course and the only examination I had ever failed in my life.

I woke up in the middle of the night and planned my sentences for demanding an analysis of my exams. "What kind of pedagogical system . . . ?" But the next day the teacher was cheery, and obviously she had nothing to do with it. I knew that any attempt to storm the central offices would be beating my head against the stone walls of French bureaucracy, one of the oldest and most unbreachable in the world. Nobody would know, nobody could or would do anything about it, and all would find my request both unheard of and incomprehensible. I let it go.

I had always been an outdoorsman, loved hiking and camping, and for many years dreamed of going to the north woods to build a cabin and live off the land. In Bergman's movie *Wild Strawberries* there is a scene where the old professor says that when he wants to calm himself and go to sleep at night, he thinks back to a scene from his childhood when his young father and mother were sitting on the bank of a lake, his father fishing with a long pole and his mother in a long white dress knitting, both smiling and nodding to him. What calms me is remembering the feeling of rightness, empathy, and contentment when I first read Thoreau's *Walden* when I was sixteen. I shivered in anticipation. I, too, would go to the woods, to live and write beside a pond.

One hot summer day when I was forty-two, I was in the back yard digging out the rotten stump of a dead elm tree. I had thrust my hands deep into the dirt and rotting wood when I felt a sharp pain, like being stabbed with a needle, in the top of the middle finger of my right hand, just behind the nail. I yanked my hand back, rubbed my finger, and went on working.

Half an hour later, I noticed that my hands were getting puffy, my eyes itched badly, there was swelling in my groin, under my arms, and behind my knees. The bottoms of my feet were swollen, and they hurt. I had no idea what was going on, but obviously something was wrong. Pat was at her dig in Kentucky, so I called a friend who came over in his car and took me to the hospital.

In the emergency ward, they gave me forms to fill out. I was nauseous. They gave me more forms. I felt awful. Finally, I put my head down between my knees and said loudly, "I'm going into shock. You'd better get me a doctor, quick!"

That did it. I had no blood pressure and my heartbeat was down to twenty-two. They put in an IV, gave me antihistamines and a shot of epinephrine. The shot of Adrenalin—epinephrine—was the magic cure. I had gone into anaphylactic shock, probably from the sting of a yellow jacket wasp. The lymph begins to separate from your blood causing hives inside and out. You can die in minutes from the shock itself, or more slowly from your throat closing up with hives so you can't breathe. A famous ancient Greek historian died of a bee sting. Far more people die of hymenoptera stings—bees, wasps, hornets—every year than from the bites of poisonous snakes and spiders and mad dogs together.

Now I carry an insect sting kit with a syringe and a shot of epinephrine. I can't remember noticing that wasps stung me before, but now they sting me all the time. I have rushed to the emergency room several times, just to wait. Nothing happened. I've let it go several times and nothing happened. Once I did give myself a shot in the woods in

Kentucky when three yellow jackets stung me on the neck. Nothing happened. Oh, the stings got swollen, but I didn't die. Sometimes you do, sometimes you don't.

"Just don't you forget," the epidemiologist said to me as I left his office for the last time, bored at having to go in for a shot every week when he wasn't certain that it would immunize me, and told me to give myself a shot of epinephrine if I got stung, just in case, anyway.

"Don't you forget that you can have a reaction and be dead in three minutes."

I don't forget. It is still soothing, however, to remember how the world and life felt to me when I was sixteen and first read about Walden Pond.


"**Y**es," Claude said, surprised that I asked. "It is usual not to get your grades back."

All that was reported on this kind of exam to determine whether a student should pass from one level to the next was pass or fail. Claude didn't understand what I wanted. I explained as a point of pedagogy that it was a bad system in which you couldn't even get a grade report on a crucial exam. Claude listened carefully. However strange my ideas seemed to him, he always did try very hard to understand what I meant.

"Ah," he said, "I see. But it is not a point of *pedagogy* at all. The exam was not given to *teach you* anything. It was given to allow *the school to evaluate* your progress."

On the last day of class at the Alliance Française, the half dozen of us still remaining made our way to a classroom in the old, main building of the Alliance Française complex. The relatively new seven-story classroom building was modern, but here the floor was of wide boards well over one hundred years old. The room was dark with narrow windows opening onto a closed court. From the ceiling moldings and beams in the floor you could see where parts of three older rooms, one of them with ceiling decorations like a ballroom, had been cut up into classrooms. We had been told to go here the day before by our teacher, who said that because so many students had gone already, classes were being integrated for the last day. Final exams were over, and it was obviously a bother that some students still wanted to go to class.

Three students we didn't know came in, and then their teacher, who was the nearsighted woman my entire class had been imposed on two months before. She was more fatigued than ever, and she looked straight through us as she addressed her own three students. It was the last day, almost no one had come to class, why didn't they just go to a café and have a conversation? Her students agreed, and they got up to go. The nearsighted teacher started to walk out, still as though she didn't know we were there.

"Hey," the Swedish girl said, "what about us?"

The teacher stopped in the doorway, but didn't look back. "I suppose you could come, too," she said with a sigh, and went on.

We did not follow. We shook hands, exchanged a few addresses, said good-bye, and went on our way.

My course at the Alliance Française was over.

**I** had always liked school. In the past when fall came, and I saw young children setting out with their books and new supplies, I felt a kind of joyful uplift that surely reflects my own childhood experiences. One week after I finished my course at the Alliance Française, school started for French children and the streets of Paris filled with their passage and chatter. I witnessed this advent with a sensation of stomach-wrenching horror. Thank God I was not still in school. I shuddered. I had been free only a week, and my inner springs of tension had not yet wound down. For the first time in my life I felt that sense of dread that before I had only heard that some children had for school. Now I was overwhelmed with frightened empathy. Actually, the children I saw seemed quite cheerful. But what if I had myself to go to school?

To celebrate my release, Pat and I went to the best restaurant in our neighborhood, Monsieur Lapin, which means Mr. Rabbit. It had no stars in the thick red guide that describes and ranks all the restaurants in France (and is a best-seller year after year), but Monsieur Lapin had very fine cuisine. The restaurant seated thirty-six, and it cost about eighty dollars for two, without wine. You had to make reservations well ahead of time, for it was full every night.

Pat and I are not good at remembering dates, and it was only the importance of not forgetting our reservation at Monsieur Lapin's that reminded us it was our thirty-second wedding anniversary.

We began with toasted goat cheese on toast. Then I had marinated gizzards and Pat had a walnut and roquefort cheese salad. For my main course I had one of the several rabbit dishes Monsieur Lapin specialized in. I was saving my centimes so I could try them all; they were delicious. Pat had something in fish laid out in an elaborate design. You notice that I have not made a study of the vocabulary of French cuisine (after all, I'm not a writer of espionage novels in which the hero always knows which vintage to order, and can tell by tasting whether they have substituted something else), so my description leaves much to be desired. I have, however, moved beyond my initial theory that people praise French food because they eat it besotted with wine.

As we were relaxing with our desserts—I had eggs-and-snow and Pat had an elaborate parfait—the lights in the restaurant dimmed, and then went out. There was a tremendous blast of ear-shattering amplified bass guitar, at the sound of which a small black poodle who had been sitting quietly under one of the tables shot out of the restaurant like a cannonball. Dogs are allowed in restaurants in France. The poodle did not slink back in for half an hour, and I was impressed by the dog's owner, who did not go after it, but continued her meal.

From the kitchen below, up the circular staircase in the middle of the restaurant, there rose a cake, flaming with candles, forty or fifty of them, held high by the waitress. She and the large party that was the source of the poodle sang "Happy Birthday." Everyone in the restaurant joined in. The waitress had changed into what appeared to be a loose-fitting suit of silver-spangled long underwear. Over this she wore black shorts and a black vest, and on her head sat a high black top hat with a fuzzy silver pom-pom rising on each side to represent ears. (Black and silver constituted the color motif of Monsieur Lapin.) She had another big fuzzy pom-pom stuck to her behind to represent a tail.

She was a thin woman. She kept her outfit on after the lights came back on and the poodle returned. Pat and I sat through it all without saying a word.

"I'm glad," Pat said about 11:30, after the cheese, when we got up to go, "that we didn't tell Monsieur Lapin that it was our wedding anniversary."

Slowly I recovered. I had been in Paris now for three months and had done almost nothing but study French. We went to the Comédie Française and to another play, and I understood most of the dialogue. We went out to dinner with French friends, and spent entire evenings speaking French.

"Look," Pat said to me, "the transformation is amazing. Before you could hardly say a word. Now you carry on conversations for hours in French."

"Last summer you couldn't say a word," Claude said. "Now you won't shut up."

I started working again in the Bibliothèque Nationale. I had a nice long chat with the woman in charge of the rare books reading room. People asked me for directions in the street and understood me when I told them where to go. I was, after a fashion, speaking French.

**D**escartes said that the ability to use language is what distinguishes human beings from other animals, known as dumb animals because they cannot speak. Even people who are deaf and dumb, even idiots, Descartes said, can manage to make some kind of noises or signs by which to communicate their thoughts. I had made it.

I went on to do some research in Holland where I attended yet another conference on Descartes. Two distinguished French Cartesian scholars were featured.

One was Professor Grimaldi, who after Professor Gouhier, who was very old, and Madame Rodis-Lewis, who was professor emeritus, was the senior Cartesian scholar at the Sorbonne and thus in Paris and thus in France, and thus, although I had not anticipated it when I started this sentence, in the world. Professor Grimaldi was a man with long arms and long legs whose bald head and naked face made him look more a Swede than a Frenchman. But the infinite variety of his facial expressions could be only French. The raised eyebrows, the enormous frown, the pinched-in closedness of eyes and mouth, and the flaring nostrils. When he lectured he needed room in front of the audience, like a high school cheerleader at a basketball game. He knelt on one knee, he turned in profile and pointed heroically to the left and then swirled to point to the right, he raised his arms out to his side and curved them on high. An enormous hand would descend to cover the top of his head, and then slide down to conceal the whole of his face except for one bulging, peering eye. The modulation of his voice was perfectly controlled, its range from shout to whisper. The stage performance itself was enough to distract me from his words, but even with close attention I could get only half of what he said. The Dutch philosopher sitting beside me, who knew French perfectly, admitted that he got only about two-thirds. "I have seen nothing like it," he said of Grimaldi's lecture, "since I was a child and went to the Reformed Church." Grimaldi should have been a revivalist, an evangelical Protestant minister. And he was in fact calling on us to confess that if Descartes was the Father of Modern Philosophy, Sartre was his son.

The other speaker was the elusive Professor Marion. He was at the peak of his form. As he spoke, I imagined him in a wig with curls tumbling to his shoulders, his hand on a sword slung at his hip, calves enclosed in a sheen of tight silk, in a stance and a sneer. It is wondrous for a bourgeois, middle-class nobody and nothing from the American Midwest, from the heart of the heart of the country, to experience the aristocratic manner. We just don't have them like that back home. He was as exotic as an elephant or a panther. He was something rare these days even in France, for although they all think well of themselves, most Frenchmen don't actually seem to know or to remember what it was in the past of their forebears that makes them so superior still today. But with Marion one could imagine that France still had a king, and that there was a court to attend. It was whispered that in his bid for the Descartes professorship at the Sorbonne, he had asked the Bishop of Paris to speak for him. "The Bishop of Paris!" someone said to me. "The man thinks we're still in the seventeenth century! He couldn't have made a more damaging move!" But a move nonetheless in the grand tradition. Hadn't Descartes dedicated his *Meditations* to the Jesuit professors at the Sorbonne? With similar negative results, to be sure. But in my estimation, Marion was unequivocally the most qualified candidate.

I liked Marion. I admired his work. He fascinated me. And as one tests again the edge of a knife on which he cannot quite believe he has just cut himself, I was drawn to speak to him again.

"Not now," he said. "Later. I am very busy."

Professor Grimaldi had won the professorship at the Sorbonne that Marion coveted. Now they spoke brightly, briefly, and turned away. But there was also Madame Grimaldi, another of those elegantly dressed, thin Frenchwomen of a certain age. She greeted Marion effusively and they stood talking animatedly. Madame Grimaldi even talked to me.

Professor Grimaldi sat centrally, languidly on a couch, keeping everyone in view. He knew who I was. "Oh, yes, Watson," he said, and turned away. At the end of the evening he once again shook my hand. He took the elbow of Madame Grimaldi gently, leaned over her, and they walked into the night. She clutched a new purse, a very fine piece of leather indeed, that she had shown to everyone. He had taken her out to purchase it that morning, her reward, her prize, her inducement, she said, for coming along.

At dinner, Marion rose to the occasion. After a taste of imported French wine and a good Dutch cigar, he dominated the conversation by doing imitations of the styles of different Cartesian scholars. If Grimaldi should have been a hellfire preacher, Marion should have been a stand-up comedian.

So there I was, in my black suit of the best English wool, seated finally in a restaurant with two top French Cartesian scholars and several Dutch ones. True, the Frenchmen had not initiated it. I had simply attended the conference and the Dutch professor in charge had casually invited me to a small dinner with the speakers afterward. A select group, he said, a little circle of Cartesian scholars. To be sure, it was in Holland, not in Paris, but, let's face it, it wasn't going to happen in Paris.

Anyway, there we were. And there, seated facing me, unable to escape at last, was Professor Marion. Now he would have to talk to me. I spoke to him at length, in French, rather well, I thought.

"Speak English," he said. And he answered me in English.

"Look," I said heatedly, "your English is just as bad as my French."

"But I am French," he said.

"Then speak French," I said.

"Are you sure you can understand?" he asked.

"Of course I can understand," I said. "I'm not an idiot."

"All right," he said, "I'll speak French. But you speak English. Don't try to speak French. Your French is terrible."

# About the Author

**R**ichard Watson is the author of many books, including *Niagara* and *The Runner* (both novels), *The Longest Cave, The Philosopher's Diet,* and *The Philosopher's Joke.* He teaches philosophy at Washington University in St. Louis.